Kathy Langley

HOW TO DEAL WITH DIFFICULT DISCIPLINE PROBLEMS

A Family-Systems Approach

By Michael R. Valentine, Ph.D.

 KENDALL/HUNT PUBLISHING COMPANY
2460 Kerper Boulevard   P.O. Box 539   Dubuque, Iowa 52004-0539

This edition has been printed directly from camera-ready copy.

Copyright © 1988 by Michael R. Valentine, Ph.D.

ISBN 0-8403-5825-3

All rights reserved. No part of this publication may be reproduced, stored in a retrieval system, or transmitted, in any form or by any means, electronic, mechanical, photocopying, recording, or otherwise, without the prior written permission of the copyright owner.

Printed in the United States of America
10 9 8 7 6 5 4 3 2 1

Dedicated to my wife, Gail,
and to my sons, Scott and Todd.

TABLE OF CONTENTS

Acknowledgements   9

Preface   11

Chapter   I.   Introduction and Historical Perspective   15

Chapter   II. Consulting with the Teacher Prior to Setting Up A Family-Counseling Session   21

Chapter   III. The Roles of the School Psychologist and Counselor Doing Family Work in the Schools   35

Chapter   IV. Other Helpful Concepts, Ideas, and Belief-Systems   79

Chapter   V.   Case Study   109

Chapter   VI. Cases   135

Chapter   VII. Questions and Answers   153

Chapter VIII. Summary   181

Appendix A: Bibliography   183

Appendix B: Parental Outline   189

Appendix C: Helpful Suggestions   193

Appendix D: Glossary   197

ACKNOWLEDGEMENTS

    I would like to acknowledge my indebtedness and appreciation to the many people whose assistance made completion of this book possible. First, I would like to thank Dr. Paul Wood, who changed the direction of my professional career by introducing me to this most powerful and interesting family systems counseling model. Second, I would like to thank Nancy Hubbell, Sue Belles, and Hugh Willoughby for their time, energy, and expertise in editing this manuscript. I am indebted and particularly grateful to Sue Leahy and Nancy Hubbell for their many ideas and suggestions to improve the book. Further, I am grateful to my wife, Gail, and my secretary, Marie Hill, who provided expert typing skills and patience throughout the many drafts of this book. Also, a special thanks goes to Gloria Inzunza-Franco for her technical computer assistance. Third, I would like to acknowledge my appreciation to the many teachers, principals, students and parents who have shared their stories and experiences.
    My special gratitude goes to Vic Braden and his staff at the Vic Braden Tennis College, who, unbeknownst to them, have saved my mental health many times by letting me work for them part-time as a tennis instructor.
    Special thanks go to Dr. Ken Weisbrod, retired Dean of Counseling and Testing at California State University at Long Beach, and Dr. James Trent, Professor of Education at UCLA. Both of these educators have had such a profound influence on my personal and professional growth and development that I feel that part of this book was completed for them in honor of the faith, belief, and trust they had in me which flamed my desire to want to become something more than I was.

And last in order, but most surely first in my heart, I give a special thanks to my family—to my parents for the love, support and encouragement they gave me throughout my life; to my wife, Gail, who patiently and understandingly supported and encouraged the completion of this goal over the past five years; and finally, to Scott and Todd, who had to wait many hours before Daddy could come out and play.

PREFACE

This book is designed primarily for school psychologists, social workers and counselors. This method for dealing with difficult discipline problems in the schools is based on a communications-based family-systems approach entitled "Brief Family Intervention".

This method is a practical, common-sense approach based on the power of clear, straightforward, direct communication and back-up techniques.

This method does not rely on psychodynamic understanding or on behavior-modification techniques. Instead, it focuses on actual parent/teacher/student communication and interaction patterns. It looks at what parents/teachers actually say and do when the student is acting inappropriately, and it compares and contrasts effective and ineffective communication and interaction patterns.

The purpose of this book is to give parents, teachers and other school personnel the ability to stop childrens' inappropriate behavior and to improve student performance in both the academic and behavioral areas.

In my earlier book, *How to Deal with Discipline Problems in the Schools,* I presented the major components of this approach, analysis of adult belief systems why children misbehave, and analysis of adult-child communication patterns. In that book the major focus was on how those components of the model could be implemented by teachers and school personnel to stop most inappropriate student behavior.

In this book the information presented in the previous book will be expanded upon and incorporated into a family-counseling model. This book will pick up where the other book

Table I. School-based Intervention Plan

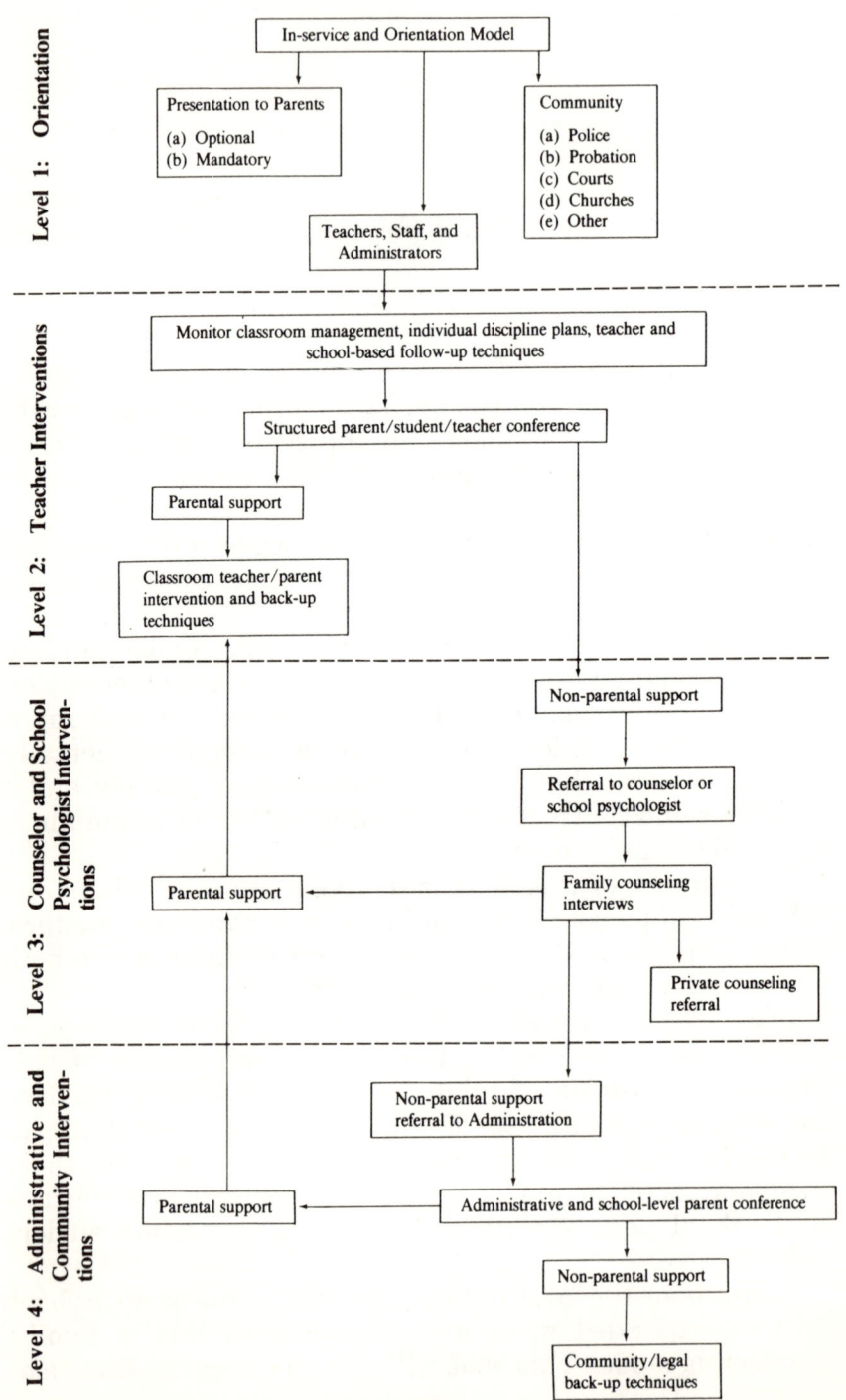

left off and will help to answer the question, "What do we do after the teachers have said it clearly, backed it up effectively, and the student still acts inappropriately?"

In Table One, a flow-chart and overview of the total program is presented. The flow-chart is divided into four levels. In Level One, a general, philosophical orientation of the principles of the approach is given to three different target populations: parents, school personnel, and appropriate community resources.

In Level Two, more-specific classroom and school-based skills, interventions, and back-up techniques are given to teachers and school personnel to increase the chances of successfully getting the students back on track behaviorally and academically.

Level Three of this model deals with the relatively small percentage of students who are unresponsive to school-based teacher interventions. Here a referral is made to the counselor, social worker and/or the school psychologist so that he/she can run a highly structured brief family-counseling session designed to have the parents see that—if they wish to do so—they can get their child to act appropriately and to do what they want him to do.

If the counseling sessions do not seem to work and the parents are unable or unwilling to get the child under control, then Level Four of the model, administrative and community interventions, is implemented.

This book will be dealing with Levels Three and Four of the total school-intervention plan. In order for you to understand this portion of the model, it is imperative that you have either read the book *How to Deal with Discipline Problems in the School,* have listened to the audiotapes by the same title, or have attended one of my all-day workshops to familiarize yourself with Levels One and Two of the program—most specifically the analysis of belief-systems and the analysis of communication patterns. These two major components are the underpinnings of the family-counseling approach. You have to be very familiar with them, and know them well, in order to use that information effectively to work with families.

Chapter I of this book provides an introduction and an historical perspective to some of the assumptions of family-systems therapy.

In Chapter II, the role of the school psychologist and of the counselor, as consultants to the teacher, will be explored.

In Chapter III, the seven steps of the family-systems counseling model will be presented.

Chapter IV explores, in a little greater detail, some of the terms and concepts of family counseling, and how they can be adapted and used with this school-based family-counseling approach.

In Chapter V, a case is presented with commentary so that the reader can see how the family-counseling model is actually used.

Chapter VI presents a summary of other cases so that the reader can get a broader perspective and see how he or she might use this approach with various problems.

Finally, Chapter VII answers specific questions and concerns which counselors have about this model and does some comparing and contrasting with other therapeutic approaches.

One last general comment in this preface: as a way to keep a consistent perspective and viewpoint, and to reduce confusion over pronouns, I have decided to refer to the counselor, social worker, psychologist, or adult as "she" and to refer to the student or child as "he". This simplification is done to keep clear, in both the reader's and the writer's minds, the interactions between adult and student/child without having to constantly change sexes or perspectives.

Chapter I: Introduction and Historical Perspective

Most school psychologists and counselors feel that the family is the most significant single influence on the development of the child. The family is the primary and most pervasive environmental structure that provides the developing human being with his or her attitudes, beliefs, values, sense of self, and related behaviors. Educational researchers have shown that both educational and personality-outcome measures, including academic performance, persistence, and self-concept, are strongly related to family background variables and interactions. (Becker, 1964; Coopersmith, 1967; Dave, 1963; Schaefer, 1972; Schroder, 1971; Thompson, 1976; Valentine, 1980).

The school system is probably the second most important environmental structure that influences the developing human being. When a student is having difficulty adapting to the school system as manifested by poor grades, truancy, acting out, school phobias, or vandalism, the school system's intervention plans have, for the most part, tried to influence the individual student in isolation from the most significant influence in the child's life—the family.

From a family-systems perspective, many of these individually oriented intervention programs (such as behavior modification, punishment, and individual or group counseling) are doomed to failure, especially if the family's influence and value system are at variance with the school system's intended behavior changes. For example, the school may try to stop a student from fighting at school, while the parent's message to the child is, "Don't let anyone push you around. Stand up for yourself." From the family-systems perspective, it is imperative that you involve the family if you wish to see more effective and enduring behavioral changes at school.

Legal implications of P.L.94-142, increased parental involvement in the educational process, and advances in the field of family-systems theory have increased the interest in family-system approaches adapted to the school setting (Petrie & Piersel, 1982). Prior to this time, school counselors and psychologists have not consistently and systematically used family-systems approaches in the school setting because they had not received training in their graduate programs, and because this approach has not been easily adapted to the school setting. Recently, however, a family-systems model (Brief Family Intervention) has been developed that is easily adapted to school-related difficulties. This model can be adapted and used by teachers in the classroom to deal with discipline problems and by counselors and school psychologists working with parents of children who are having difficulties.

Before getting into the specifics of the family-counseling model in any great detail, a general and brief introduction to some of the philosophical and historical perspectives of family-systems therapy might be helpful.

Historically, most psychologists have looked at inappropriate behavior in students from an intra-psychic, one-person, and/or medical model. They assumed that some process or intra-psychic phenomenon inside the child's brain caused him to act inappropriately. They believed that if they could get inside his head and change whatever was going on intra-psychically, they could change the child. This intra-psychic phenomenon could be any belief, attitude, perception, or emotion. They tried to work with the child, usually in individual counseling or therapy, to change his inappropriate behavior. Using a medical-model analogy, they tried to do some type of therapeutic surgery to fix these maladaptive, intra-psychic perceptions or beliefs. Even if they believed that the family had something to do with the child's behavior, they usually worked with the child individually. This orientation prevailed even in group counseling. In group, they dealt with one person at a time as if the problem were intra-psychic and in isolation from the family context. Even if they used some of the other group members' influence and experience to help change one person's perspective, they basically saw the individual as having the problem and dealt with him in isolation from the family context.

Behaviorists, who generally reject the intra-psychic and medical models of human behavior, also, however, operate primarily from a one-person model, and typically see the child as the one with the problem. They bring all their research and behavioral technology to bear on this identified patient and try to shape, extinguish or reinforce certain targeted behaviors. Again, this attempt is usually done in isolation from the family context and dynamics.

Family-systems theory brought about a major theoretical shift from a one-person, intra-psychic model to a multi-person, interactional model. Psychologists using the family orientation no longer look at the child in isolation. Instead, they look at the total family configuration, and in some cases, even the environmental context (*e.g.*, schools), to see how these contexts affect the child's behavior. The child is no longer seen from a one-person model in which he is the problem, or even from a two-person model in which the child's problems are seen as an interactive effect between two people (teacher/student, mother/son). Instead, the family-orientation model sees the child's behavior as a function of the interrelations and dynamics of at least three people. To illustrate the difference in the perspectives of the various models, I will paraphrase a story told by Jay Haley, a famous family therapist. From a one-person model, a teacher talking to a student who was not doing well would say, "The student is stupid." If she operated from a two-person model, the teacher might say, "There must be something about my personality (*e.g.*, I'm too domineering) in interaction with this student that inhibits him and makes him appear stupid." If she operated from a three-person model, she might say, "The student is caught between two different approaches, ideas, orientations, or beliefs—mine and those of teacher X; not knowing which to adopt, and not wanting to offend either of us, he seems confused, uncertain, and inhibited."

Many times, from a family-systems perspective, the symptom-bearer, or identified patient (I.P.), is seen as (1) being caught between two opposing positions, or (2) having to set up a very tenuous coalition with one of the two opposing positions—a process which inevitably leads to rather unfortunate and destructive outcomes.

From a systems perspective, the counselor needs to be trained to look for various coalitions that might take place among any groups of three or more (*e.g.*, mother/father/child parents/child/school, family/school/hospital, and so on). One of the working hypotheses which you should test out any time you have a student who doesn't seem to respond to your school-based interventions is, "Who in the system is in coalition with the child or is supporting the child in the continuation of this behavior?" The assumption is that the child does not have enough power on his own to continue to act inappropriately if significant others expect him to stop. Therefore, you have to find what power-base the child is lined up with to help maintain the behavior. Another way of expressing this is, "Whose shoulders is the child standing on?" Going back to the previously mentioned example of the student fighting, it becomes clear that the student is standing on the father's shoulders, and receives support with statements like, "Don't let anyone push you around. Stand up for yourself. Be a man."

Understanding what a person does, or what his or her motives are, becomes quite different as one shifts from the individual to the broader context in which that person functions. From this new vantage point, psychopathology or dysfunctional behavior is seen more as the product of a struggle between persons than as between internal forces within a single person.

This movement away from the intra-psychic perspective to an interpersonal, family-systems perspective might appear to be a minor shift, but the implications are profound in the fields of psychology and education. Because of this shift, we no longer see the child as crazy or emotionally ill. For all practical purposes, we've wiped out most psychological jargon, nomenclature, and diagnostic categories. We now simply say that the child is acting inappropriately, and we need to put a stop to such behavior. Rather than trying to analyze intra-psychic phenomena, we look at the interaction and communication patterns between the child and the parents and/or teachers. We analyze actual interactions that can be seen and changed. It is assumed that if you can change the interactions within the family system, then you can change the child's behavior, and eventually, the subjective, intra-psychic, phenomenological experience of that child. From the family-systems perspective, the child is no longer seen as the only one with whom we work. We want to look at the broader picture—the family system. In so doing, we are not looking for causation or for blame: we are looking for what is actually going on in the family's interactions, and for how the family can change these interactions if they wish to do so.

Within the field of family-systems theory, there is a wide range of philosophical and theoretical orientations that choose to emphasize different aspects of family life and dynamics to account for behavior and change. It is not my intent to summarize the various family-therapy models. If you wish more information in this area, I refer you to Goldenburg and Goldenburg, 1980; Jones, 1980; Levant, 1984 for overviews of the field of family therapy. These references, as well as other significant books in the field of family therapy, are found in the bibliography in Appendix A of this book. Suffice it to say, this particular model, Brief Family Intervention, falls more within the framework of what many systems theorists call "the communication systems purist perspective". This particular model and perspective assumes that what people actually say is a reflection of what they mean, of the way they see the world, and of what they believe.

The Brief Family Intervention model is based on communications theory, which suggests that words reflect a concept. Most of us are familiar with the classic linguistic illustration of the word "snow". For most of us in our western culture, "snow" basically has one meaning, and only one perceptual reality. Eskimos, however, have more than seven words for various types of snow, thereby creating over seven different perceptual realities. Therefore, the word helps to define the concept, the belief, and the reality.

Beliefs and concepts about the world are linked intrinsically to our choice of words, interactions, and communication patterns. For the most part, we act and communicate congruently with what we believe. Therefore, if we wish to change the way we act and communicate to children, we must examine and question our beliefs about the causes of student's inappropriate behavior. It is the contention of this book that if most of the popularly held beliefs of why students misbehave were objectively examined, little or no evidence would be found to support these beliefs. Success at objectively evaluating, challenging, and eroding these popular beliefs would then leave open the possibility of communicating and acting in a totally different manner. Such changes in beliefs and communication patterns would then set the stage to quickly stop most of the student's inappropriate behavior.

The logic of this system is simple: if you believe that the student is incapable of doing what you want him to do, then you will not directly and clearly tell him to do what you want him to do. For example, if you believe that a student is hyperactive and unable to sit still, you will not tell him to sit still. Such a direct statement is incongruent with your belief that he is hyperactive and unable to sit still. However, if the belief-system is challenged by objectively collecting evidence, and thereby proving that the student is in control of his behavior and is capable of sitting still, then it becomes reasonable and congruent with the new way of seeing things to tell the student in very specific and concrete terms to sit still. This new way of seeing the student as capable then enables the direct communication patterns or statements to be backed up, if need be, with actions that convey to the student that he is to do as he is told.

One of the important skills of this method is the development of questioning techniques that allow the teachers and parents to see that their belief-system has nothing to do with the causation of the inappropriate behavior and that they have actual observable evidence to prove this fact to themselves.

To use this model effectively as a consultant to teachers, or as a counselor to families having difficulty, it is imperative that you know how to analyze beliefs and communication patterns well. I suggest that you re-read and familiarize yourself with Chapters II and III in the book *How to Deal With Discipline Problems in the School,* and then practice with some of your colleagues at eroding typical beliefs that you have heard over the years.

Chapter II: Consulting with the Teacher Prior to Setting Up a Family Counseling Session

Referral from the Teacher

Your first step as a counselor or a school psychologist is to set up an appointment with the referring teacher to discuss the problem. As a consultant to the teacher, you are interested in determining what the teacher's goals for the student are and what actual intervention patterns took place. More specifically, you want to know what the teacher actually said and did in response to the student's inappropriate behavior. You are looking for breakdowns in the interaction patterns between the teacher and the student which might have allowed the student to continue to act inappropriately. Examine the communication interactions carefully. What was the sequence of the interaction? What did the student say and do? What did the teacher say and do in response? What did the student do then, and what did the teacher do in response to that? Stay with behavioral, observable sequences so that your inquiry provides a clear picture of what took place.

If the teacher says the student has a poor attitude and refuses to do the work required, ask her what the student actually did or said that gave her the impression that the student had a poor attitude. What would the student need to do in order that if he did it, she would no longer feel that he had a problem? Ask when the student refused to do the work, what did the teacher actually say to him to get him to do the work? When that didn't work, what did the teacher do and say then? You have to ask questions that will help the teacher to: (1) clearly define what the problem is in very specific concrete terms; (2) clearly state the goals of the intended intervention so the teacher will absolutely know if the student is back on track, is successful, and if the intervention worked; and (3) see and understand the actual sequence of communication and interaction patterns between her and the student.

Steps One and Two are linked together. If the problem is not clearly defined, then you will never know if it is solved. Conversely, if the teacher's goals are clearly and specifically stated, then the solution to the problem is usually obvious, and you or any other observer would know if the standards were met and the problem was solved.

Having teachers state their goals for students in descriptive, observable, specific terms is not as simple as it seems. Most teachers describe student behavior in vague, indirect, abstract, inferential, trait-attribute, judgmental terms. They say things like, "John is very aggressive," or, "Sue is immature and very shy." These statements are inferences, presumptions, and judgments rather than descriptions of observable behavior. Getting the teacher to use descriptive statements of behavior is a necessary first step in working toward a solution to a problem. Think of how you might question, and work with a teacher who described a student as "unmotivated", "lazy", or "aggressive". Ask the teacher to describe what she saw (*i.e.,* observed) the student doing that led her to believe that the student was "unmotivated", "shy", or "aggressive". Ask, "Are the assignments and work not started on time?" "Is the work not completed?" "Is it not turned in on time?" "Is it turned in all wrong and sloppy?" "Does the student volunteer to answer questions during discussions?" "Does the student hit other students?" And so forth. The answers to these questions should be statements that describe what the student is doing, or not doing, which can then be easily translated into intervention strategies that can solve the problem. For example, it is much easier to devise intervention strategies for a student who doesn't start his work on time, or a student who lays his head down on his desk, or one who pushes into line, than it is to devise solutions for an "unmotivated" student. Describing student behavior in observable, descriptive terms also helps teachers to clarify the issues in their own minds, and helps them to decide what they are going to say to the student about the issues (*e.g.,* "Get to work right now." "Do the problems neatly and correctly." "Start immediately, and have them completed in the next fifteen minutes.").

By helping teachers to define the problem and by clarifying their goals or solutions to the problem, it then becomes relatively easy to get the teacher to see and understand where the communication patterns have been breaking down.

In Step Three, if you get a clear behavioral understanding of the actual sequence of communications, then you can help teachers to understand this process by comparing and contrasting actual communication patterns of times when they have been successful in getting their students to do what they wanted with those times when they have not been successful. An example of this process that I gave in the first book bears repeating.

A first-grade teacher consulted with me about an "immature, acting-out" little boy who wouldn't do anything she wanted him to do. When asked what he did that led her to believe that he was "immature and acting-out", and what she had tried in order to prevent him from misbehaving, she replied that every time she gave directions, he whistled. At first she ignored the behavior, hoping that it would go away. She then tried several tactics: "Good little boys don't do that when I am giving instructions"; "If you keep that up, you will have to stay in during recess"; and, "Now, class, let's all turn and look at John, and when he is finished whistling, we will begin." None of her approaches worked.

"What did you do when you had had all you could take, and when you got really mad at him?"

"Well, I wasn't feeling too well, and he was really bugging me. Finally, I just said, 'Stand up right this minute, clean off your desk, put your chair in, go outside, stand on this side of the door where I can see you, and whistle until you get tired of whistling. Then you may come back in this classroom.' "

"Did he do all the things you told him to do?"

"Yes. He stood out there and whistled for over fifteen minutes. The only problem was that he was up to his old whistling tricks again after a few hours."

At this juncture, it was pointed out that she had been successful in getting him to do exactly what she had told him to do—go outside and whistle. Yet, in attempting to stop the classroom whistling, she did not tell him directly and emphatically, "Stop whistling, and never whistle again in this classroom."

After consulting with the teacher, and if it is found that she did not follow through with appropriate communication patterns and/or back-up techniques, you can provide suggestions for stopping the student's inappropriate behavior. You might work with the teacher to design an individualized discipline plan for that particular student (Review "Individual Discipline Lesson-Plans" either in the workshop *Workbook,* pp. 41, 42, or in the book *How to Deal with Discipline Problems in the Schools,* pp. 92-93.). You may also role-play and practice the interventions so that the teacher knows what to do and is well prepared for any eventuality. (Review Chapter Five, pp. 88-95, on "Individual Discipline Lesson-Plans" in the first book. If you would like, you also can listen to a demonstration of this process on Tape 5, Side B and Tape 6, Side A of the audio-tape series entitled "How to Deal with Discipline Problems in the Schools.")

You should also ask the teacher whether or not she has conferred with the parents of the child. If the teacher has not contacted the parents, you might suggest a structured parent/teacher conference, and then work with the teacher to prepare for that conference. (Review the "Structured Parent/Teacher Conference", Chapter 5, pp. 95-110, in *How to Deal with Discipline Problems in the Schools.*)

If the teacher appears to be saying and doing the right things but is still having difficulty with the student, you may ask the teacher if you could observe what is going on in the classroom, or depending on your knowledge of the teacher, just accept the referral and contact the parents. Many teachers, after having worked with this model, want you to observe them in the classroom, first to verify that they are communicating clearly, and secondly to see if they are backing up their words with effective follow-through.

If you go into the classroom to observe, pay attention to the non-verbal as well as to the verbal communication. Notice the tone of voice, the facial expressions, and the gestures of the teacher; the physical distance between the teacher and the student; the concreteness and specificity of the message (Are there loop-holes for the junior-lawyer types?); the intensity level; and the use of appropriate back-up techniques.

When working with teachers in a consultant role, remember that you are colleagues working together to solve the student's problem. You are not doing therapy, so stay away from anything that delves into the teacher's personal issues. In a consultant role, for the most part, never erode teacher belief-systems or get into the teacher's family-of-origin issues; stay with the actual communication and interaction patterns and back-up techniques employed to stop the inappropriate behavior. For the most part, erode teacher belief-systems on a group basis, such as at staff development or during in-service days. However, if you know the teacher well, and you sense that she can take it; that she is really interested in growing and understanding; and that she trusts you and your helping style, then you may very cautiously question some of the evidence they have about the assumptions or beliefs which she has about the child's inappropriate behavior.

Remember, however, when working with peers, that it is better to take your time and develop trust and a good long-term working relationship first than to be "right", have them see the errors of their ways, and have you lose the battle, because they won't work with you.

As a way to illustrate some of the points that I've been discussing, I would like you to read the transcript of an interview which I did in front of a teacher group attending a summer training-program at California State University, Long Beach.

Listen carefully to what the teacher said and did and see how the actual words she used became a reflection of some of her belief-systems. This interview was not designed to show counselors how to consult with teachers. It was used as a demonstration interview for teachers with the intent of leading into a class presentation on the different belief-systems and communication patterns. Even though this interview is not how you would work with teachers as a consultant to classroom behavioral problems, the structure and the format of this demonstation interview is very similar to some of the things that you might do in a consultant role. As you read the interview, see if you can put yourself in a consultant role and ask yourself, "What would I ask her?" Or, "How would I work with her to get her to see how successful she is in certain areas and show her the different principles, techniques, and communication patterns she has used when she has been succesful and when she has not?"

Counselor/Teacher Demonstration Interview

Interview: Teacher = T
            Counselor = C

C: What's your first name?
T: Carrie.
C: What grade do you teach, Carrie?
T: Second grade.
C: And your student's first name.
T: Tommy.
C: So Tommy is a 2nd-grader; and what is he basically doing that is causing a problem? (*State the problem and* set the goals for the solution of the problem; help the teacher to clarify and operationally define the terms.)
T: He has a very *short attention-span* and has difficulty *staying on task* with any given assignment. (These terms need to be defined.)
C: When you say a "short attention span", what do you mean exactly by that?
T: Because he would begin a task and then immediately leave it and go on to something else.
C: Okay. So your definition of a "short attention-span" is that he would start something, not complete it, and go on to something else.
T: Yes. (Now the problem can be operationally defined—completing an assignment on time, neatly and correctly, rather than trying to solve "short attention-span" or attentional deficits.)
C: He does this quite regularly?
T: Yes.
C: What was the other thing you mentioned? Short attention-span and something else? (I forgot "difficulty staying on task".)
T: Along with that, he has an *inability* to focus on a given assignment or task for very long. I guess the two would be interrelated, and when he gets frustrated and can't do

something he will immediately turn to another child and start antagonizing him, maybe pulling hair or hitting. (Two possible beliefs: (1) "inability to focus", and (2) if he is "frustrated", he has to let it out.)

C: So the child is also hitting and pulling hair and acting inappropriately.

T: Yes.
(In this role, I didn't explore setting the goals to solve the problem, but I did clarify some problem areas up to this point—not completing assignments, hitting, pulling hair, and so on. If I were working as a consultant, I would start moving in, getting very specific and concrete, prioritizing the problems and setting goals.)

C: Okay. What are your ideas, your hunches, on why he is doing these types of things? (I'm interested in making some of the beliefs explicit. I'm not interested in eroding them. I'm interested merely in showing that beliefs have a bearing on what we do and say. I'm not doing therapy with the teacher.)

T: Well, we were just told earlier not to relate to the social or to the home environment. (The professor teaching the university class had told the teachers they had no control over outside influences, so only focus on what is going on in the classroom.)

C: Don't worry about what anybody else has told you. What do you really think causes some of the problems?

T: I know. But that was what I was thinking, too. The child has a very difficult time at home. I know his mother does drugs, and a lot of time the kids come to school without having had breakfast. It's a really bad situation there. I attribute some of his behavior in class to this. I believe that you cannot separate the home environment from the school environment.

C: So, basically you believe there are some types of home enviromental issues—possibility of drugs, not having breakfast, poor mothering that might account for his behavior.

T: Right. (I'm not interested in trying to erode the beliefs in this situation. I'm interested only in showing that the beliefs one has have a bearing on what one will do and say.)

C: Okay. Any other hunches, of why he's doing what he's doing that have crossed your mind?
T: I think that he has some psychological problems, too, that. . . .
C: Emotional problems?
T: Yes, emotional problems. The school psychologist has been working with him on getting him into a special class.
C: Have you also thought of the possibility that he might be hyperactive, have an attentional delay deficit, or anything like that?
T: Yes, he does show some hyperactivity. He shows some real intelligence as far as strong oral language goes, but he still at this grade level has the inability to write a complete sentence and to. . . . (Some people may think that I am leading the teacher with this type of questioning, but as can be seen later, teachers usually tell you if they really think that the things which you bring up are important or not. Again, the intent is just to list beliefs at this time, so I keep her focused, and cut her off from going into great detail about the beliefs. Also, be sensitive to the use of the word "inability". She has used this twice, and this may reflect other possible belief-systems.)
C: But that has crossed your mind, at least as a possibility of what has caused part of the problem. Okay, anything else? You have the family, you have the possibility of hyperactivity, and you have the possibility of emotional problems and this type of thing. Anything else?
T: . . . .
C: What about the possibility that he is a boy? Is that just the way some boys are? (Possible belief—boys will be boys—remember, make the implicit, explicit.)
T: No. No. My other boys aren't like that.
C: That's not a possibility?
T: No. (Teachers will tell you if something is not an issue. Don't worry about leading questions.)
C: Now, what have you actually done with this youngster? When he messes up and goes over and hits somebody, pulling hair; what have you done and said to him when he's done this? What have you tried? (Get examples of actual communications.)
T: Well, I've told him basically that. . . . I follow a lot of Canter's assertive discipline: "Tommy, you can choose to

continue working nicely at your seat, or you can choose to leave the room, sit by yourself, or go work in the principal's office."
C: So you give him an if/then contract.
T: Right.
C: What else have you said and done? Do you remember?
T: Well, positive reinforcement, too: "Tommy, if we can finish this much, if you can complete *just one sentence*, then I'll let you have some free time or you can come up and get a candy." (This message tells the child indirectly, "I don't believe you can finish this assignment, and I'll be surprised if you actually finish just one sentence.")
C: So then, that's the same type of thing, a positive if/then contract.
T: Right.
C: Now, when he is actually hitting a student, what have you done? Is there anything in particular that you have said? What do you do to break up the fight? (Get more specific, and get actual examples.)
T: Well, I ask him "why" he did that. And he says, "Well, he took my pencil or did this or that," and I realize that because he is a *special child* that a lot of the times the kids will antagonize him. (Another possible belief—he is a special child.)
C: So, basically you're asking him 'why' he is fighting? (If you were working with this teacher to help to clarify the problem and to develop better interventions, you might initially ask her just to get the process going, "If he tells you a good enough reason 'why' he is fighting, is it okay for him to continue to fight?")
T: Yes.
C: Does that work? Does that stop the behavior?
T: Well, he at least gets to have himself heard. He gets attention. (Another belief-system—he needs to be heard and get attention.)
C: But he stops fighting?
T: Yes, he usually does.(I should have asked, "If he doesn't stop, what do you do and say?")
C: But he goes back and fights again the next day?
T: Oh, yes!
C: So what do you do the next day?
T: Basically the same thing. Ask, "Why are you doing this?"

C: Do you ever have a day when you have really had it with this kid? (At this point, push the conversation to see what she does and says when she has had it with the child. See how she has been successful at stopping the inappropriate behavior at Point Ten when the child is "out of control", or successful at punishing the child in some amazing way.)
T: Many days!
C: When you've had it up to here, what have you said and done then?
T: Get the h___ out of my classroom!
C: Does he leave?
T: Yes. I really lost it.... (I didn't want her to continue about how she "lost it", or trying to justify her behavior. I wanted to stay with the fact that she got the student to do what she said, namely, "Get out of my class.")
C: And the student did leave then?
T: Yes, he did. I had my aide take him up to the office.
C: Helped him out, huh?
T: Escorted him.
C: Backed it up and made him do it. (She said it clearly, meant it, and backed it up. It worked.) Okay. Just out of curiosity, were you ever like this youngster in any shape or form when you were going through school? (At this point, I know she can be successful if she wants to be. I need to look for the reasonableness of her actions and look for any other possible beliefs or transgenerational issues that might account for her behavior.)
T: I was like that tremendously. That's how come I can relate to the kid.
C: You were.
T: I can remember many instances where I had a difficult time staying on task and had a difficult time following instructions.
C: How did you react when teachers did certain things to you? Were there certain teachers that you really didn't respond to?
T: Oh, yes.
C: Give me some examples.
T: I had a third-grade teacher, Mrs. Morgan, who would get very angry, very mean when anyone displayed that kind of behavior. So she was very frightening.

C: And so did you ever say to yourself, "If I'm a teacher, I'll never be like Mrs. Morgan?"

T: Oh, yeah, tremendously. Even my fifth-grade teacher I am thinking of, too. I have even gone back and talked to him. He's still teaching at the elementary school where I went and I always had a difficult time with his abruptness and his behavior toward students. I said, "If I ever become a teacher, I will never treat a student like that." But at the same time, even though we say we would not want to be like that, we still end up doing so. I believe *our human nature* dictates to us sometimes, and we still do those things even though we feel they are inappropriate. We still sometimes lose it and do it. (She knows the incongruencies of what she wants, versus what she does. She tries to justify it by a rationalization or belief: that's just the way human nature is. If you can get teachers to get students to do what they want them to do, then teachers don't have to worry about incongruencies and justifying having "lost it".)

C: Did you feel crummy about it after you did it? (This was not phrased well. I was trying to show her that even though she "knew" better, had insight and understanding, she was still trapped in a vicious circle of acting incongruently, which made her feel guilty and ashamed even though she wanted to act differently.

T: Oh, yes, I felt crummy. (She knew. At this point there was no need to go into greater detail on this issue, because I understood where she was coming from—from past school experiences. I wanted to see if there was any parallelism to possible family of origin issues. This was somewhat awkward because I didn't want to get too personal in front of the class. I felt, in many ways, that she had already revealed a little too much.)

C: What about in terms of your own family? I assume that you might have had the same types of things—somebody in your family—maybe someone's style of relating to you and your inability to "stay on task"? Did you not care for the way a particular member—your mom or dad?—tried to handle you? (I just love having a way with words—where are they when I need them?)

T: My mom. I didn't enjoy the way my mom would discipline me as a child.

C: Okay.
T: Are we going to have a psychological analysis? (Too close to home. It is time to get out of this the best way I can.)
C: (laugh) No we're not going to get into anything like that. I just wanted to see if there were any typical or general patterns. . . .
T: I hated my mother; I loved my father.
C: (laughs) I think that's basically all I need to know at this point. I'll back up and make it clear as to what I was trying to do.
T: Okay.
C: Thank you very much for helping out.

I think it can be seen from this interview that this teacher's beliefs about the child's problems and her own educational and family experiences have clearly affected her communication and interaction patterns with this student. Her interventions and communications, for the most part, have been *reasonable* based on her personal philosophy of life and education, as well as her belief that the student was incapable in various ways. However, the thing to remember is—even given this understanding—that when she really wanted something to happen and she meant it, she was capable of getting the student to do what she wanted. Under this success condition she clearly communicated to the student and backed up her communication with actions. In my mind, this points out her ability to be successful in other areas as well, if she would be willing to use some of the same principles of success in the areas where she is having difficulty with the student. The successful communication and back-up interventions become even clearer when you compare these to her indirect, vague "if/then" statements and "why" questions.

In summarizing the discussion in this chapter, when consulting with teachers:
1. always have them clarify in specific, concrete, descriptive terms exactly what the problem is;
2. have them set goals that clearly state what the solution to the problem will be;
3. have them tell you exactly what they have said and done in attempting to solve the problem;

4. find out where they have been successful at getting the student to do what they wanted;
5. compare and contrast the different communication patterns and back-up techniques they used while being successful or non-successful;
6. help them to develop an individualized discipline plan which prepares them for most eventualities; and, if need be,
7. help them to prepare, or role play for a teacher/parent/student structured conference.

Finally, if the student fails to respond to appropriate actions by the teacher, something else is probably working to keep the inappropriate behavior operating. At this point, then, it is necessary to call the parents for a family-counseling session.

Chapter III: The Roles of the School Psychologist and Counselor Doing Family Work in the Schools

The counselor or the school psychologist faces unique problems in running a family counseling session within the school setting. First, as a specialist, you must define your role as a helper in a different way. Even though you are being paid by the school, you must divorce yourself as much as possible from the school's and the teacher's position and work from the family's perspective. You are a family advocate—not necessarily school or even a child advocate. The teacher and the other school personnel will not change their rules, and they have very specific goals in mind for the student, so don't worry about having to defend, uphold, or support their position. Be an advocate for helping the family.

As a family advocate you will help the family to clarify their values and position relative to the school's stated goals, and you will help the parents to see that they are capable of changing the child's behavior if they wish to do so. You are not the "heavy" who tries to force the family to change or to adopt the school's position. While you do not necessarily have to agree with or value the family's position, you must consider parents to be capable of getting their children to do what they want them to do and operate from their perspective, not from yours. You must be non-judgmental. Again, your job is to help them to clarify their position in relation to the school's stated goals and objectives. With this orientation, you will help the parents to *see* that they are capable of changing the child's behavior, if they so desire. Philosophically, you must understand that up until this point the parents have not changed the child's behavior because either they valued the behavior, they felt that they shouldn't or couldn't interfere as parents to change the behavior, or they held erroneous beliefs that the child was incapable.

When parents see that they are capable and successful at changing the child's behavior without the counselor directly telling them to change that behavior, they are placed in a compromising position. When the parents and the child understand that the parents are already successful and can change the child's inappropriate behavior if they want to, then the parents are forced to take a stand and make their position clear. They either want to change the inappropriate behavior, or they don't. If they choose not to change the child's behavior, they have provided a clear message to the child, to the school, and even to themselves that they value the inappropriate behavior and actually encourage it.

In using this model, you will operate from a few basic tenets. In so doing, you may have to challenge some of your own beliefs, as well as some of your professional training. The first tenet is that parents are very capable of getting their children to do what they want them to do. The counselor or psychologist must orient himself/herself to seeing and believing that parents are capable, and should look for parental strengths and talents instead of weaknesses. For some therapists this perspective is initially difficult, especially if they have been trained in intra-psychic, individually oriented psychology, or psychopathology, in which the child is perceived, in most cases, as the victim of bad parenting.

Most family systems approaches see everyone in the family as part of the problem and as a victim of the problem, or at the very least as a part of the maintenance system that sustains the inappropriate behavior. At times, you might need to fight your natural tendency to side with the child because you see him as the victim. At these times, remind yourself that you have little or no influence in changing this child's life. The family has the power and influence to change the child's life, so you must work with them to get them to see that they are capable of change.

If you want to help the child, align yourself with the parents to help them to see their strengths and capabilities to change the problem behavior. Do not get trapped into blaming the parents. They probably already think that the problem is their fault and feel uncomfortable about having to come to you for help. Put them at ease and operate from the perspective that it doesn't really matter how the problem came to be. What is going on in the family at this time is what you must deal with. Look for ways to change the present problems. Do not look for blame or causation, but rather look for the strengths and resources which the family has to solve the problem.

Jay Haley, a famous family therapist, has an apt analogy: A car gets a flat tire without the driver or its passengers necessarily causing the flat. Together, everyone in the car can work quickly to solve the problem, without blaming each other. If they channel their resources in the right direction, they can get on with their lives.

Sometimes counselors, who may themselves have had troubled family backgrounds, find it hard not to blame the parents. But unless you are willing to be a second parent to this child, you do him a disservice by siding with him against his parents. Ultimately, even if the parents "deserve to be blamed" for all the injustices in this child's life, it serves no therapeutic purpose to blame them. When a parent becomes defensive because he is being blamed for the problems, there is little hope for change. On the other hand, if you can enter the family system with the least possible resistance, help create a positive atmosphere of strengths and capabilities, and move the family toward more adaptive functioning, then the possibility of change is much greater and you serve the welfare of the child in a more encompassing way.

Even when one of the parents appears to be "emotionally disturbed" or lacks "good parenting skills", you still need to look for strengths and get both parents to take a stand to help their child. If such a situation arises, more time and energy may be needed to look for their strengths and capabilities, but they are there. It may require some imagination and creativity on your part to relabel perceived parental weaknesses as strengths. But this relabeling will help the parents make a stand to correct the child's inappropriate behavior.

This relabeling of perceived deficits as assets is exemplified by the position often taken by Rational Emotive therapists when confronted with an individual who is acting in a rather strange and bizarre way. The therapist indicates to the person that he must be a superior learner, as demonstrated by the fact that he has learned to act in such ingenious, creative, inappropriate ways. Since he is so adept at learning and is obviously a superior learner, the therapist is sure that the client can change his behavior and learn new more adaptive styles of meeting his needs if he wishes.*

Even though you perceive the family as capable, you still have to be realistic in terms of the amount of change which you can expect. Some families have major problems, and you will have only limited time with the family when you work within the school setting. This book deals specifically with short-term interventions done in the school setting, and in so doing, it necessarily reflects limitations of time and scope.

As a counselor or school psychologist, you will always be faced with tight time limitations; you will be lucky to get one, maybe two family sessions, three at most, to effect some type of change. If the family seems to be having extreme problems in many areas, you must consider this particular school-based intervention as only one part of a therapeutic intervention and refer the family to outside agencies or therapists. No matter how many problems the family has or how apparently naive or narrow your interventions are in relation to these bigger problems, you need to emphasize to the parents that you know that they care about their child; that they are successful in many areas in the family; and that in spite of other family problems, they can take an active stance to help ensure the child's success in school.

A second basic tenet of this model is that the child is seen as capable of doing what he is requested to do. The child isn't seen as sick, crazy or emotionally ill, or incapable. (This model doesn't deal with childhood schizophrenia, or autism. It deals with typical behavioral and acting out problems found in most child guidance clinics and schools). The child's behavior is simply seen as *inappropriate behavior* that needs to be stopped. The behaviors that schools require of students, especially in the discipline areas, are relatively simple and well within the ranges of the child's capabilities (*e.g.,* don't talk when the teacher is giving instructions, line up to go outside, don't hit anyone, raise your hand and get permission before you, . . . and so on).

It may sometimes be difficult to see the parents and the child as capable. Some parents and children are so good at

---

*For more about relabeling and reframing, see Jim Alexander's *Functional Family Therapy,* Brooks/Cole, (1982), or Salvador Minuchin's *Family Therapy Techniques,* Harvard Press, (1981).

sending up smoke-screens, acting crazy or irresponsible, that it is difficult to see their strengths and resources. Compounding this rather natural tendency to see the worst in people, we often have to question our own professional training which teaches us to be psychological sleuths, looking under a therapeutic microscope for the tiny cracks in a individual's personality armor. However, once you have had some success with this approach and actually see how capable both the parents and the children are, and how even the child's extreme acting-out behavior can serve a purpose in the family, you will find it easier and easier to look for capabilities rather than for psychopathology—to perceive people's strengths rather than their weaknesses.

The third tenet is that there are individual temperament differences in children. Some children are relatively easy to rear; others are much more difficult. The crucial issue is not so much that there are temperament differences but rather that there are differences in the amount of *structure* necessary to ensure that each child acts appropriately and is successful. Some easy-to-rear children require only a simple request to get them to do what you want them to do. More-difficult children initially require more-specific directions and stronger back-up techniques to make sure that they are equally successful.

Chess and Thomas's research on temperament differences shows that right from the moment of birth there are tremendous differences in children's temperaments.* Some parents will have more difficulties than others because of the child's temperament. A counselor or a school psychologist can understand and empathize with these parents while at the same time getting them to focus on the issue: does the child need to master the task that the parents are requesting of him? If so, they need to do everything in their power to make it happen. With this particular child it may initially require more time, energy, structure, guidance and supervision, but if it is important, then they must do something about it.

This concept of differences in children also appears in other areas such as intellectual differences, learning style dif-

---

*Chess, S., and A. Thomas. 1963. *Behavioral Individuality in Early Childhood.* New York: New York.

ferences, and energy-level differences. The same general principles in relation to different amounts of structure, guidance, and involvement to assure success apply in these areas as well. To give a simple illustration, some children are toilet-trained easily with little intervention, modeling, reinforcement, or structure; others take much more time and training. The issue to note is not the differences, but how the task is viewed. When the task, such as toilet-training, is viewed as important, natural, traditional, or functional, it is amazing how the majority of people achieve that goal in a relatively short period of time—no matter what the individual temperaments or intellectual differences of the trainees.

The fourth tenet is that children, for the most part, misbehave for one of three basic reasons: (1) they procrastinate (just as adults do); (2) they have learned that they can get away with it, or eventually receive some payoff; and (3) they're trying to clarify the family or social structure (find out whom they can count on to provide structure, guidance, and support). These last two reasons for children's inappropriate behavior are the leading causes for families' and teachers' having difficulties. In many ways the role of the counselor is to assist the family to see how the child is requesting help for and clarification of the family structure. Sometimes, inadvertently, the parents and the school let the child get away with inappropriate behavior and even reinforce it because no one takes an active stance to clarify the child's role and position or to prevent his inappropriate behavior.

With these four basic tenets, or orientations, coupled with the analysis of belief-systems and communication patterns presented in the book *How to Deal with Discipline Problems in the Schools,* the therapist is ready to call the parents for a family-counseling session. It is absolutely imperative that the counselor or school psychologist has committed to memory the various ineffective communication patterns presented in Chapter III in the previously mentioned book, and has actively practiced questioning and debating various, possible, erroneous parental beliefs, such as those presented in Chapter II of the same book, before attempting to run a family counseling session.

Calling the Parents

Your next step after clarifying the problem with the teacher is to inform the parents that their child was referred by the teacher. When you call them, tell them the reasons for the referral in specific behavioral terms, and indicate a willingness to be of help if they so desire. Ask the parents if they would like to set up a meeting to deal with the teacher's referral. In those rare situations in which the parents choose not to see you, try to persuade them in a positive, supportive, non-demanding way. Remember that you are offering a service to the family if they wish to avail themselves of it, so don't demand a meeting or put pressure on them. Teachers and principals can pressure them, your job is "just to help". The attitude which you wish to convey to the parents is that you are a family advocate; that even though you are an employee of the school, you are there to help them to *see* that they are capable and have tremendous positive strengths and resources to change behavior if they wish to do so. However, if all of your positive persuasion does not work, indicate to the parents that you will be available for a future conference if they change their minds. Emphasize that you care about the well-being of their child and are there to help the family.

At this point, tell the teacher and the principal that the parents choose not to see you at this time and that if the student does anything wrong, they should immediately suspend him to parental supervision. This suspension is not designed to change the child's behavior so much as it is designed to force the parents to work with the school. Ask the teacher and principal to "help motivate" the parents to come to school and clarify their position in regard to the student's inappropriate behavior. The principal's pressure and the student's suspension to parental supervision should force the parents to work with the school and most especially with you, the counselor. If necessary, let the administration play the "bad guy" role and you play the "nice guy" role. Whether the parents come to see you of their own free will or under duress makes relatively little difference because in either case you will have to establish as quickly as possible your third-party, family-advocacy role, deal with their initial resistance or reluctance, and tell them that you are there only to help them to *see* that they can solve the school problems if they wish to do so. You are not there to make them do anything. Once the parents are in your office, either by choice or pressure, it becomes a matter of how quickly you can put the family at ease and establish yourself as a third-party helper.

Typically, when you call the parents, they wish to resolve the problem and are more than willing to see you. Make an appointment for a meeting that includes both the parents and the student. Some parents will say that both of them cannot be there at the same time because of work, or that they would like to meet without the child present. You must insist that all parties meet at the same time. Sometimes one of the parents will say that he/she can't get the other parent to come in or that he/she isn't sure why the other parent has to be present. Tell this parent that to solve the problem you must understand each person's perspective. Stress that by working together as a team, you will all be able to solve the problem more quickly and more effectively. If that approach doesn't work, tell the parent that if he/she cannot persuade his/her spouse to come in, you will be willing to call the spouse and explain why it is so important that all of you meet at the same time.

Another possibility is to demonstrate to the reluctant parent how a problem affects everyone in the family, not just the child. Notice how the following conversation chains the interaction sequence:

Telephone Conversation: M = Mother
                         C = Counselor

C: When John gets into trouble at school, how do you find out about it? (John's problem)
M: The school calls me at work.
C: How does that affect you or make you feel?
M: It makes me angry. I'm the one that always gets called and has to go to the school to solve the problem. I'm running the risk of losing my job, you know. (John's problem becomes her problem at work.)
C: So you're pretty upset and are running the risk of losing your job. When you get home, what happens? (Continuing the sequence.)
M: John and I talk about what happened at school. It always ends up in an argument, both of us get upset. I usually

send him to his room until his father gets home. (Problem at school becomes problem at work becomes problem between Mom and Son at home.)
C: So the problem at school carries over into the home, and both of you get upset. What does Dad do in this situation?
M: I usually meet him at the door and let him know what John has been up to.
C: How does he react to all of this?
M: He gets mad. He gets mad because he always has to come home to problems. He gets mad at me because I "don't handle it right". Then we always seem to get in an argument. (Problem at school becomes problem at work becomes problem between Mom and Son becomes problem between Mom and Dad.)
C: What does Dad do then?
M: He storms around and goes into John's room and raises Cain with him. (Now it becomes a problem between Dad and John.)
C: It sounds like the problem John is having at school affects everyone in your family. (Probably even other children. In private practice, you would want to bring in the other children on the initial visit, but in the school situation bring in only the student and the parents.) It affects the emotional atmosphere in your family, and everyone ends up feeling pretty hurt and upset. Everyone seems to lose. One of the reasons I want both parents to come to the meeting is so we can stop John's inappropriate behavior, help to prevent this sequence of events, and use all of our resources and talents to develop strategies so everyone's needs are better met and no one loses, gets hurt, or feels left out.

Do whatever is necessary to get everyone to the meeting. Remember that if you can't get both parents and the student together, you drastically reduce your chances of changing the inappropriate behavior of the student and increase the chances of having the left-out party sabotage the best-made "intervention" plans.

When divorced parents are both actively involved in the parenting function and are amenable to working together in the student's best interest, both parents should be present. If one parent is not in the geographical area or is out of the family picture in terms of the parenting role, you may see one parent without the other, as long as the parent seen is willing to take over the major parenting functions, and you realize that issues about the missing parent must be dealt with and made very clear in the session.

Sometimes the parents wish to see you separately from the child to "fill you in about the child". It is important to meet together so that everyone knows what everyone else has said, thereby reducing any paranoia, secrecy or miscommunication and also increasing the chances of success of the behavioral changes. If the parents suggest that they want to talk about a certain topic without the presence of the student, such as the student's stealing, you can ask, "Does the student know that he is stealing?" The parent will say that he does. You can reply, "Since it is no secret and he knows, there is no problem with all parties meeting together to help to resolve the problem."

If the parents want to talk about personal information about the child that is basically irrelevant to the school problem, (e.g., his sex life, personal habits, and so forth), tell them that although you understand the importance of that information, it is beyond the scope of the school's involvement. Tactfully cut them off and refocus their attention on the school-related problems. If it appears that there is a long history of negative family interaction which is beyond the scope of the school-related problems, offer private counseling referrals. However, do not use other family problems as an excuse for not dealing with the school problems. No matter how involved and complex the previous family history, the parameters of the school-related problems and interventions can and should be delineated and focused on. The counselor should prevent the parents from wandering off the topic or abdicating their responsibility to help to solve the school-related problems because of other family issues or problems.

Remember that the student must be present at the session to hear what is said and done because when the parents' belief-systems are eroded, the foundation is laid for change—not only for the parents but for the student as well. When the student hears the parents explore their belief-systems and give contradictory evidence to erode these beliefs of his incapability, he will have a chance to challenge, explore and relabel his own subjective constructs and labels. This encounter will help him to grow and develop, especially if he later goes into individual or group counseling. (See example in Chapter VI, pp. 140-143.)

Having the student in the session is crucial if the parents send mixed messages, or if they send hostile, rejecting messages. At the very least, you will be able to clarify what is going on within the family and make the implicit, explicit.

If the parents send rejecting messages, you should ask them if this is the actual message that they wish to give to the student: "Are you saying that you hate this kid, that you don't want him in the home anymore, that you want him to leave and never come back? Or are you saying that you care about him, but you are so frustrated, angry, and hurt by some of his behavior that you are not sure what to do anymore and you feel as though you would like to kick him out?" When asking questions, always put them in an either/or style so you don't back the parents into a corner. However, be prepared to go in either direction with the parental responses.

In extremely rare situations—and I would like to stress *extremely rare* situations—if the parents reject the child, and after you have tried other manuevers to get the parents to make a positive stand, be prepared to get outside child protective agencies involved in the case. Even though this parental rejection is initially very painful for the student, it (at least in some ways) clarifies his position in the family: his parents don't care about him and cannot be counted on to provide structure, guidance, and support. Once that message is clearly understood by everyone involved, you and other outside agencies will have to work intensively with the student to help to support him and encourage him to initiate individual change and responsibility. In the long run, the student will be better off to discard the delusion that his parents do care about him even though they are psychologically, and possibly physically, abusive. In a rare situation like this, you must make referrals to outside agencies to coordinate efforts to support this child. You also need to file against the parents for neglect. On the other hand, if the parents say that they are hurt and frustrated, you can use their reply as a way to introduce an open discussion of their fears, concerns and interaction patterns. You'll be able to relabel any previous name-calling and negative labels in a more benign way and work with the parents to set limits, give clearer messages, and effectively back up their rules.

Family Counseling Session

When the family first comes in, introduce yourself to each member of the family. Spend a short period of time socializing with the family. Right away look for family strengths, or positive or unique assets that you can identify with. Set yourself apart from the school as much as possible and try to join the family as one who is interested in the family's well-being and as one who identifies with parental concerns. Try to reduce any tension, anxiety, or defensiveness. If it feels comfortable and *the situation warrants it,* you can disclose that if you were in their position, you might feel a little bit apprehensive about being there, or possibly being blamed or seen as bad parents. Immediately, assure them that you're not looking for blame. If anything, you are looking for solutions, and you are glad to be working with them because they are the most important and influential people in their child's life.

If the parents are there under duress, let them complain a little. Listen to their concerns, empathize with their feelings, and help to clarify the issues. However, as you do this, channel their attention to the reason for the meeting: you're there only to help them *see* that they are capable of solving the problem if they want to do so. Guide them in a discussion of the problem as they see it. Get them to focus on the problem and a solution to that problem. If the parents focus on the student as "the problem", and they wish to vent their anger and frustration "on him", always intervene early in the initial interactions. Do not let them dump negative history on you or on the student. If necessary, interrupt them politely and refocus their attention on solutions to concrete solvable problem behaviors. Tell the parents that you understand he has been a problem in the past; however, you are concerned with what he needs to do now, so that if he does it they will think he is no longer a problem.

Let the parents know, again only if the situation warrants it, that you're not there to make them do anything. You are there to help them *see* that they are the most important influence in their child's life and are very capable of changing the child's behavior if they wish to do so.

If it seems appropriate, you might wish to give a brief introduction to what you do, your role and why you wanted everyone there. For instance, you might point out that the problem affects everyone; together everyone can help by using their unique strengths and resources to help solve the problem quickly; everyone will hear everything said so that there will be no miscommunication; everyone will know what the intervention plan is and will be better able to work together as a team to solve the problem without getting angry or fighting amongst themselves; and the solution to the problem will come much faster and be more successful, thereby reducing the chances of the school always "pestering" the parents at work.

After explaining why it's better to have everyone present for the family session, describe the chain of events which caused the meeting in the first place. The teacher referred the student to you for.... You called the father and asked him to come in with the family. While on the phone, you basically said.... Indicate that the purpose of the meeting is to discuss the family's perspective of the problem. Describe what you know of the problem and how the school perceives the problem. After you describe the situation, lead the family into a discussion of how they perceive the situation, and *whether or not the behavior in question is a problem to them.* Many times, however, in my own counseling sessions, after a very brief socialization phase, depending on the time and my sense of parental strengths, I just ask the parents what seems to be the problem and thus get right into it. Without directing your questions to anyone in particular, ask what the problem is. Use this indirect inquiry as a diagnostic probe. Many times (but not always) the parent who does the most talking and complaining—the parent who will answer your questions first—is either overly involved with the child in an unproductive way or has less power to change the problem than the other parent has. You have to assume that if the complaining parent had the power, he or she would have changed the behavior by now. This is often the case, but you also have to be careful not to jump to this conclusion because sometimes there **is just a family rule or tendency for one parent to be the spokesperson.**

After this brief socialization and introduction, you are ready to go through the steps of family counseling. If you are just learning the model, it may be helpful to take notes during the session. Table II gives an overview of the model and can help to structure your note-taking.

Table II. Therapist's Guide: Outline for Therapy

Step 1: Setting the Goal
What is the problem?

Step 2: Analysis of Parental Beliefs

____ Hyperactive	____ Heredity
____ Emotional illness	____ Deprivation
____ Ignorance	____ Defective models
____ Brain damage	____ Phases or stages
____ Socioeconomic status	____ Normal behavior
____ Wind and weather	____ Demanding too much
____ Marital problems	____ Other beliefs

Summary and comments about beliefs:

Step 3: Analysis of Communication Patterns
What have parents actually tried? Use actual examples. Be as specific as possible, using the parents' actual language:

Step 4: Areas of Parental Success
Give actual examples:

Step 5: Summarizing the Session:

Step 6: (Optional) Any need for review from parents' perspective?

Step 7: (Optional) Have the parents practice what they are going to say and do while in the office. (Develop a back-up lesson plan) See Appendix B.

As a counseling strategy, in and of itself, taking notes slows the interaction down. If you are just learning to work with families, taking brief outline notes might enable you to follow the interactions better. It also helps to structure the session if you get a chaotic family that overwhelms you with too much information at once. You can say, "This is very important. Let me write this down. Let's see, first you said . . ., then this happened." Taking notes can be a way of maintaining focus and structure while at the same time validating, respecting, and joining different family members' perspectives ("so you see the problem this way and feel..."). When you want to stay on a particular theme or even stay with a particular family member's perspective when others are interrupting with new information, you can say, "That's an important point; let me make a note of that so we can come back later to clarify it, but right now I want to. . . ."

Don't be afraid to take notes as a structuring aid to help you work with the family. Most people are generally mystified by note-taking, and they accept it. (We're never really sure what the physician is writing in our file when we go for an office visit, but we assume that it is important, and usually the note-taking doesn't bother us.) Also, you can use your note-taking to give yourself more time to consider where you want to go next. The therapist can say to a family, "Let me see if I understand this...", or "Let me see if I have this straight...." Then the therapist "reviews" his notes, not really concentrating on them but instead focusing his mind on what he wants to say and do next.

Family Counseling

The following seven steps are meant to provide some structure for you as you learn this particular family-counseling approach.

Step One. *What is the problem, and what is the solution? Setting the goal of the counseling session*

After the preliminary introduction and orientation, have the parents set the goal of the counseling session. Setting the goal requires stating clearly both the problem and the desired behavior change, using observable, behavioral terms. Clear goals ensure that everyone in the room knows what the problem is, what will be required to resolve the problem, and what the criteria for success will be. Setting clear goals is usually more difficult than it seems and requires you to take an active, directive role. Always remember that even though you are being paid by the school system, you have to operate from a family-advocate position; your own values and those of the school are not at issue and should not interfere with your family-advocate position. Your job is to actively clarify the parents' statement of the problem so that when the final goal is agreed upon, everyone in the room will know exactly what the problem is and what needs to be done to solve that problem—whatever that might ultimately end up being.

Even when a parent begins with an observable behavior, it is important to clarify the nature of the problem.

Parent: Brian is truant from school. I've gotten two calls at work in the last week.

Counselor: How is that a problem for you, and if it is a problem, what needs to change so that you'll feel there is no longer a problem? (To some parents, truancy is not a problem. It is the fact that the school keeps calling them at work that is a problem.)

Whenever a parent mentions that a student is getting straight F's, some counselors will jump to the conclusion that this is the problem and try to deal with that issue right away. Don't assume anything. As a standard operating procedure ask the parents, after they have described the student's behavior (he is getting straight F's, he's on drugs, he stays out late), "How is that a problem to you, and what would you like changed so that when it *is* changed you will think that he is ...?"

Sometimes the parents initially tell you what others have reported to them as the problem since they perceive you as "part of the school". Listen for, and develop a sensitivity to, "canned" answers. When you hear one, convey to the parents in a non-judgmental way that it is no problem to you if the student does the particular behavior because you are only there to help them, not the school or other authorities. Ask them, "Is this behavior really a problem to you, and if so, how? What would you like changed?"

To elicit an honest definition of the problem, you might want to use a mild shock treatment. Identify yourself with a position opposite to the one a traditional school authority figure would take.

Parent: He is getting straight F's.
Counselor: I know a lot of people who got straight F's in high school, and they turned out fine. How is that a problem to you?
Parent: He is flunking out of school.
Counselor: Edison and Einstein flunked out, and they did okay. I know many guys who flunked out of school, went into the service, came back, and did fine in college. I have also known students who have flunked out and have not done well. How is this a problem to you, and what would you like to do about it?
Parent: He is cutting classes.
Counselor: I know some very respectable families that say that cutting classes is okay with them. The parents figure that they get to take mental-health days from work, so why shouldn't the kids be able to do the same thing? In fact, in some cases, they even write excuses for the students. How is cutting classes a problem to you?

When parents use vague, abstract terms, you need to identify and clarify them. Make the vague specific and the abstract concrete.

Parent: I really feel that Susan has a poor *self-concept*. She has a *bad attitude* toward school, and she is not working up to her *potential*. (The italicized abstract terms are too vague to be useful. Neither the parent, the student, nor the counselor will know when the stated goal has been met under these communication patterns. Terms like these need to be actively clarified.)
Counselor: Let's take these one at a time. What is Susan doing that leads you to believe that she has a *poor self-concept*? What behaviors must she do, so that when she does them you will think she has a good self-concept, a good attitude and/or is working up to her potential? When you say she is not working up to her potential, what does she need to do to convince you she is working up to

her potential? Would straight A's or B's be working up to her potential? What are the standards that must be reached so that when she reaches them, *you* will know, *she* will know, *everyone* will know, that she is working up to her potential?

In this way, the counselor helps to modify the parents' communication pattern and directs the parent to state the goal in observable, behavioral terms. Even at this point, the counselor may have to assist the parent in defining the desired behavior.

Parent: She's making mostly D's in school, and I know that she's capable of doing better. I never see her doing her homework. If she would just *try* to get better grades, I'd think that she was working up to her potential.

Counselor: When you say, "Try to get better grades", do you mean that she *has* to get better grades—no choice—or can she just try, and if it doesn't work she can quit? How hard does she have to try? If she keeps trying for the rest of her life and still gets D's and F's, is that okay with you? When will you know that she has tried enough and is "working up to her potential"?

These questioning examples are intended to provide several ways of clarifying the desired behavior. You will, of course, use your own clinical skills and ask questions in an empathic manner to clarify the issues and to understand exactly what the parents want their child to do.

In this first step, the counselor *actively* clarifies each parental statement so that the "how", "when", "where", "for how long", and "to what degree" becomes concrete, behavioral, and specific. If the parent states that the child has to do his schoolwork, the counselor should inquire about specific standards: How long must he continue to do it? A week? A semester? Until he graduates? In all subjects? To what standard of excellence? 75% right? 90%? 100%? And so on.

Often, the parents will introduce a number of problem behaviors.

Parent: He is truant, flunking out of school, smoking marijuana, talking back to his mother, stealing, and punching his sister.

You must ask the parents which issue is the most important to them and the one they really want to work on first. Begin with what they believe is the biggest problem or the crucial issue. Once the parents successfully handle the most pressing problem, they will feel capable of dealing with the other "less significant" problems. It is important that you let the parents—not the school—select the most pressing problem because the issue is not the "problem" itself but having the parents go through the problem-solving process to discover that they are capable parents. In accepting the parents' choice of the major problem, you demonstrate respect for them as the most significant people in the child's life. If you get the parents to successfully solve the problem which they consider most crucial, you thereby enable them to see that they are very capable of changing the "less important" school problems if they wish to do so.

Don't worry, though: most parents will choose to solve the school-related problem. It is usually the main reason, and the only reason, that the parents are there. Most parents believe that their child's education is very important, and they want the best for their children.

However, if the parents choose a problem other than the school problem, you will have to decide whether or not to deal with the problem within the school setting. You must consider the family and the nature of the problem, the constraints of your time, the school's philosophy and policies, and the scope of your training and expertise. If you feel comfortable and the school is supportive, work with the family. But if necessary, refer the parents to outside family counseling. Even if you make referrals, suggest to them that if they desire, they can take a first step to help correct some of the other issues in the family working on one specific school-related problem. Try to refocus the situation on the school issues and see if the parents are willing to work on those.

Many times, all the problems cluster around one or two key issues, and if you can deal with those, you can solve other problems at the same time. If you have the flexibility to work with the parent's goals, you may be able to solve the school-related problems in the process. For example, a student is getting F's, is truant from school, goes to a friend's house, smokes marijuana, is involved in minor theft to support his pot habit, has a bad attitude at home, and lies about most of his truancy, smoking, and stealing. In setting the goals, the parents begin to tell "war stories" about how awful the student is. Politely cut them off, and prevent them from counterproductive complaining. Focus their attention on defining the problem and the therapeutic goal. If the parents begin by saying they cannot trust him anymore, focus their attention on what he must do to regain their trust.

Keep clarifying the parent's thinking until you focus their attention on the key problem.

Parents: Well! If he would just stop lying about everything.
Counselor: If he continues to get straight F's, cut school, smoke pot, and steal, would that be okay with you as long as he told you the truth about it?

The parents may then focus on the stealing and pot-smoking because they believe that he steals to support his pot-smoking, which in turn leads to cutting school and getting poor grades. Even if the parents' top priority is to stop the pot-smoking, the clustering effect forces the other problems to be included. The parents may solve them all as they develop the structure necessary to get him to stop smoking pot. For instance, as a first step to help ensure that he will not smoke pot, they will need to stop him from going unsupervised to his friend's house during school hours. In effect, they will need to solve the truancy problem in order to solve the pot problem. By solving the truancy and the pot problems, they will help to solve the straight-F's problem. In setting the parents' top priority into a workable goal, keep in mind that the other problems can probably be worked into the plan to ensure achievement of the major goal.

Many other parent-education programs and intervention strategies assume that parents need to be taught what to do and suggest beginning with the simplest problems and generalizing to the more difficult ones after initial small successes have been realized. This program, on the other hand, assumes that parents are capable of tackling the toughest problems first. (If you would like further information on a different way to change behavior without assuming that parents are incapable and need to be educated, I refer you to Jay Haley's book *Ordeal Therapy,* Chapter Four.)

Sometimes, parents try to push the decision-making onto you or the child. At times parents sound very convincing when they say things like "He is 16 years old; he should know better. He needs to be responsible for his own actions." At this point, you must be firm and insist that the *parents* reach an agreement regarding the desired behavior change. This decision must not be left to the student. It has been left to the student in the past, and it has not worked. If it had worked, they wouldn't be seeking help! (For more information on this position of not leaving the decisions up to the student, I recommend Jay Haley's books *Leaving Home* and *Problem-Solving Therapy.*)

In reply to the parents' contention that the child "should know better", you may say, "Yes, I agree with you; he *should* know better, but he has demonstrated to you very clearly that he does not know better. He has not gone to school for the past two months and has gotten straight F's. Evidently, this is no problem to him. Since it is no problem to him that he flunks out of school, and it appears that he is willing to be responsible for that, is this behavior a problem to you, the parents? If so, are you willing to do something about it?"

In some instances, you may have to force the situation to get the parents to make a decision.

Parent:	He's 16 years old; he needs to make these decisions himself and be responsible for them. Besides, I can't make him go to school.
Counselor:	Well, if you can't do anything about it, and if it's his choice, then get off his back and let him get straight F's, and flunk out of school. I would suggest that you learn to love him for his independence and just hope for the best.
Parent:	I can't; he's got to get a good education—life is tough these days.
Counselor:	Then do something about it. What do you want him to do?
Parent:	But I can't make him do it.
Counselor:	Then don't. Let him flunk. If you can't make him and he knows that, then it will never happen. So

let him flunk and become a failure, and learn to love him for it.

Parent: But I can't let him fail. I love him, and it is important to get a good education.

Counselor: Then do something about it. What do you want him to do, so when he does it, you'll feel comfortable again?

It is hoped that by using this type of manuever you will help the parents to clarify what needs to be done, and help them to take a stand to make it happen.

As mentioned earlier, the parents need to agree on the problem and on the behavioral standards for the solution of the problem. Sometimes a lack of agreement *is the problem,* and you get the sense that the parents do not agree on anything and that they are sabotaging each other. (Mom says, "Straight A's". Dad says, "School's not that big a deal.") At this juncture, be very empathic and non-blaming but very directive. Tell the parents that it is important that they get together as a team, coming to some type of agreement on at least a minimal standard acceptable to both. Only in so doing will they be able to support each other to make the child successful at school. Remember that you are not interested in marital therapy, so keep the focus on the student and what the *parents* can do to help him to succeed.

Keep in mind that the parents' behavior is reasonable based on their beliefs. Part of your job is to find out what those beliefs are, challenge them in a caring, supportive way, and point out that even reasonable beliefs sometimes contribute to a student's inappropriate behavior. I've known fathers who will not make their sons go to school, not to undermine the mother's influence, but to avoid being like their own fathers who were authoritarian, abusive and dictatorial. These fathers, in their efforts not to be "like their fathers", let their children make their own decisions. If you find the parents' action (or inaction) to be a result of a "reasonable" belief, then question the belief, debate it, and put it into a different context. Point out the reasonableness of the father's actions but also point out how the student's undesirable behavior is a consequence of this reasonableness. Ask questions like, "Do you want your son to be a failure?" "Can you give him some clear directions, set limits and make him do certain desirable behaviors without being authoritarian, abusive, or dictatorial like your father was?"

Another technique to dramatize contradictory messages from the parents is to turn to the child and say in a very firm voice, "Get up out of this chair, go out in the hall, and sit there until I tell you to come back." The student and the parents are initially stunned by this maneuver, yet usually the student will make an attempt to leave the room. As soon as he makes an attempt to leave, tell him, "Sit down—and don't move until I tell you to." Then, quickly repeat your first command telling him to leave. By this time, the student is totally confused. At this point ask the student how he felt and what he wanted to do about it. Usually the student feels confused and unsure about which command to follow; he thinks you're crazy, and he just wants to forget this whole weird counseling business. Now, you turn to the parents and say, "Your child has been confused and unsure about which direction to follow in your family. He has been getting two messages, probably for reasonable, legitimate causes, but two just the same: to go to school and get good grades, and the other that school is no big deal." Unfortunately, no matter which of the two conflicting messages the child follows, he loses the love and support of one parent. Ask the student to come sit by you (a symbolic maneuver to get the child out of being caught between two different messages) and just listen to the parents as they discuss the issue and see how they come to some resolution of the problem. Direct the parents to discuss this issue with each other and come up with a reasonable, mutually agreed-upon message that they wish to give to the student. This message must be one that they will both support. You may have to enter into the discussion with some therapeutic maneuvers to help the parents to come to a conclusion. In some families this non-agreement may be the whole problem and its resolution could effect a wide range of outcomes.

When parents are having marital difficulties, even contemplating divorce, you must confront them empathetically, but directly. Ask them if they are planning to divorce themselves from the child. Ask them if they are willing to work together and support each other in this area of the child's educational welfare even though they have personal differences and/or problems in their marriage. An agreement between the parents will help to clarify the child's position in the family and enable rapid change to take place. Even if there is a divorce in the family, the parents can still agree and support each other in relation to the child's education. In some cases, the mother, the step-father, the father and the step-mother have all come together and agreed to support each other in this one area to ensure the educational success of the student. Don't be afraid to clarify the issues; more often than not you will find support for the student's well being.

Unfortunately, some parents refuse to agree to work together to help the child. This situation, as unfortunate as it is, will, however, help to clarify and make explicit some of the family problems and give direction to the issues needed to be addressed in the session. Under this unusual situation, you can push the parents to make a stand in the best interests of the student. Be direct. Tell them that their actions are putting the student in a weakened position, and if they do not take action, there may be dire consequences. Paint a graphic picture of the consequences as you perceive them. Bluntly ask them if this is what they wish for their child, and, if so, to tell him now so he will know that they want him to be a failure. This technique gets their attention, and usually gets them to take a less ambivalent position and to start working on the problem. However, if you use this maneuver, you must be prepared for the opposite reaction. In rare instances the parents may tell the student bluntly that they wish he had never been born, and as far as they are concerned, he is a failure and always will be. Have back-up support-systems ready to help the student through this crisis. At this time, get private counseling for the family and the student, and bring in child-protective agencies and other professional organizations to help the child. If this is not just fleeting parental frustration and the situation in fact cannot be resolved, help to remove the child from the family setting.

This may seem like a drastic measure. However, a student who lives in an uncaring, hostile environment under constant threat of emotional and physical abuse suffers devastating, long-lasting effects. The student would be better off if the parents make it clear that they don't want him. Even though the loss is initially devastating to the student, it can be dealt with directly and realistically—like a death in the family. Once the student knows the "rules" of the family and gets over the initial stages of grief and loss, he can be more realistic and get on with his life and make good therapeutic gains.

Another issue that sometimes arises in this first stage of counseling that needs to be addressed is unrealistic parental expectations and demands. Generally, parental expectations and demands are reasonable; however, you need to question and clarify everything. If you think that their expectations may be unrealistic, question them. Ask the parents what evidence they have to support their belief that their son should get straight A's. Has he ever gotten them before? Has he been tested? If so, what were the test results? What do his teachers say about his ability? If the parents give you evidence that he is very capable, continue your line of questioning and find out what they are willing, if necessary, to go through to reach this goal.

Counselor: It sounds like you have overwhelming evidence to support your position. I know that parents are capable of getting their children to do what they want when they put their full effort into it. So, there is no doubt in my mind that you can get him to do what you want him to do. The only question I have is whether or not you have thought about the trade-offs to achieve this goal. If your son does not wish to get straight A's, which his behavior indicates, how much time and energy are you willing to invest to make it happen? For how long? Are you willing to monitor his behavior for as long as it takes? Are you willing to run the risk that he might hate this and put up a fight?. How much strain will this put on your marriage? What about his social and emotional development? Will he have any time for fun—sports, music, dating, and other activities? What do you really want for your son in all these areas, and what can he realistically achieve, given the time and circumstances?

Continually ask questions until you are satisfied that the goal is realistic and that the parents understand what achieving the goal might entail. Theoretically, if a parent was setting unrealistic demands and was willing to take the responsibility for the consequences of those demands, there is not much the counselor can do to change that. If that is the case, the counselor can help to frame the parents' actions within the context of a scientific experiment, a diagnostic probe, or data-collection on a trial basis to see how things go. The counselor can help the parents to develop monitoring systems and intervention strategies so that they can effectively reach their goal. Then, check with them periodically to see how they are doing. If they are successful, they know their child better than the experts did. However, because you helped to frame this as a scientific experiment, a diagnostic probe, if they are not successful, they are free to readjust their goals and continue to work with you if they wish.

Don't worry; extremely high, unrealistic parental expectations are rare. Most parents are happy just to get their more-than-capable children to obtain straight C's rather than the straight F's which they have been getting.

In brief summary of Step One: Focus on a specific, observable behavior problem that can be solved; keep the family focused on the solution to the problem rather than on finding causes or affixing blame. Do not accept generalities or abstractions for the counseling goals. If you don't define everything in concrete terms, the later therapeutic process will fall apart. Strive for clarity and memorize the communication patterns so that you can actively clarify the parent's intentions in setting the goal. (*E.g.,* "Do you *want* him to go to school, or *must* he go to school—no choice? Do you want him to *try* to get to class on time, or *must* he get to class on time? When you say, 'No ditching school', does that mean under all circumstances? When you say that he is immature, what does he have to do so that when he does it, you will think that he is mature?") As I said before, this first step initially sounds very easy to do, but it usually is not so easy as it sounds. It is absolutely imperative that the counseling goals and solution to the problem be stated clearly and specifically—because if they are not, you and the family will have no idea if the interventions really worked, and you will probably get sidetracked or lost in the later steps of the counseling process. It's like the old saying, "If you don't know where you're going, you're likely to end up somewhere else."

Having made the goal very clear and having reached agreement on the problem and the solution to the problem, the family and counselor are ready to begin Step Two.

Step Two: *Analysis of Belief-Systems*

In Step Two of this model, the counselor explores why the parents believe that the child is not doing the desired goal behaviors set forth in Step One. This step involves skillful questioning which allows the parents to see that their beliefs of why the student is not doing the goal behavior may be flawed. In addition, the counselor has the parents bring out specific, observable evidence to prove their own beliefs invalid. The ultimate way to determine that a belief is erroneous is to prove that the child is capable through observable evidence. Have they ever seen the child do what they want him to do? If they have seen him do it, then the child is *capable,* and they can forget all the excuses (beliefs) that they have previously entertained. Review the chapter on "Analysis of Belief-Systems" in the previous book and become familiar with some standard questioning techniques for the more popular beliefs. [Chapter IV of this book also has additional examples of parental beliefs that you need to become familiar with.] Plan ahead and prepare questions for particular beliefs that parents typically bring up so you can "spontaneously" move through the session.

Again, be active and directive in your questioning and in your challenges to the parents' beliefs. This is not Rogerian "Uh-huh" therapy. You do not have a year to "build trust and get to the problem". You have one, maybe two sessions. While you don't need to be abrasive, disrespectful, or impolite, you do need to be clearly goal-directed and assertive. You are the director, and you must guide the interactions. When parents say,"It's all those rotten, good-for-nothing kids down the street that make him steal, take drugs, and cut school," you may ask, "Why do you believe your son has no backbone and can't say 'no' to these people? Has he ever *not* followed the crowd? If so, how do you account for the times that he does and the times that he doesn't? How did he get to be this way? Did he learn it from Dad? From Mom? Why is he such a follower?" Ask the boy directly, "Does anyone make you cut class? How did they do that? Did they drag you off fighting and screaming? Have you ever *not* done something some other student or person tried to make you do?" If so, ask, "How did you do this if you are such a follower?" Ask the parents, "How do you account for this if he is such a follower?" You have to be prepared to follow the parents' line of thinking wherever it might go, and continually ask for what evidence they have to support that contention.

Or the parents may say, "The reason the boy does what he does is that he is hyperactive and can't control himself." (Always ask the parents to describe and define for you in very behavioral terms exactly what they mean by hyperactivity, and then have them describe exactly what the boy's behavior is.) Ask them, "How do you account for this? Minimal brain damage? Blood-sugar level? Biochemistry? Or is there another cause? Does he ever sit still? Under what circumstances? Does he sit still when the teacher is right beside him? The mother? The father? The principal? Does he act the same at school? In your home? On weekends and weekdays? At the dining-room table? Watching TV? At the neighbors? At the grandparents'? In church? In court?" If his behavior changes under these different circumstances, how do the parents explain that in terms of biochemistry, blood-sugar level, or any other reason? "Does he have two different biochemical systems—one to turn the sugar on and one to turn it off when Dad is around? Please explain that? How does that work?"

No matter what the parental belief is, it is important to find out what evidence the parents have to support that belief. Furthermore, you must make the parents realize that this belief has nothing to do with the student's inappropriate behavior or at the very least cast a doubt in their minds and, just as importantly, a doubt in the student's mind. You create doubt by pointing out inconsistencies in the parents' beliefs and by pointing out specific observable evidence that the child can control himself.

As is common in counseling sessions, sometimes the real issues, motives, or beliefs don't come out immediately. This approach is no exception. Occasionally, the parents don't bring up some of the "real" beliefs or reasons why the child is doing what he is doing until they trust you and feel that you can help them if they really open up. Therefore, you must develop a rapport with the family by respecting them and by not judging their beliefs and values even as you question the validity of some of their beliefs. Communicate a sense of respect for the parents and encourage them to reveal the real reasons why they believe the child is doing what he is doing. Be directive but very empathic; use your clinical experience and hunches to help draw out these beliefs and to dispel them as excuses for allowing the child to continue his inappropriate behavior. Remember, this is short-term counseling (one or two sessions), so be more directive and develop techniques to get at the real problem quickly without being pushy or discourteous. Use your sensitivity: watch the family for clues to see if you're going too fast or are losing them. Be aware of the paradox here. You must get at the parental beliefs, erode them, and in essence dismiss them. At the same time, you must do it in a caring and respectful way, communicating to the parents that the belief has been reasonable up to this point. If you do this skillfully, they will trust you with their reasons for why the child is acting inappropriately, thereby enabling you to tell them that these beliefs are no longer viable excuses for continuing to let the child act inappropriately.

Besides eroding erroneous beliefs, you should try to make the implicit explicit; help create an open, non-threatening environment in which important issues can be talked about. By doing so, you help to set the stage for later individual counseling with the student if it is needed. (A case example of this technique is given in Chapter VI, pp 140-143.)

Here are some pointed questions which you may wish to ask if the parents don't bring up some of these issues in some form or another:

Is your son stupid?
  Does he know what he is supposed to do?
  Does he have special learning problems?
  Is he emotionally ill or crazy?
  Does he have deep emotional problems that he can't control?
  Are you or your husband lousy parents; do you blame each other for the student's problems?
  Is there something medically, genetically, biochemically, neurologically, or anatomically wrong with the student?
  Are drugs and/or alcohol related to the problems in the family?

By drawing issues out, you clarify for the child issues that he or someone else in the family may have been thinking, feeling, or acting upon. For example, when you explicitly ask the parents the mental health status of their child, you can dispel the hidden or implicit message that everyone who goes to a counselor or psychologist must be emotionally ill or crazy. If the parents deny the belief, and you openly discuss the possible fears or worries associated with the issue, you help to dispel the child's implicit fears and worries and you set the stage for future change. If the parents say, "Yes, he is crazy," ask them what evidence they have to support their position and then thoroughly discuss that issue.

When you ask if drugs or alcohol are related to the student's problems, phrase the question in an ambiguous manner. Don't directly ask, "Is your son on drugs?" Instead ask "Are drugs or alcohol related to the problem?" This question could mean "Is the student on drugs?", or it could mean "Is Dad an alcoholic who comes home and beats on his family?". When you ask the question, watch the family closely. Look for subtle signs that tell you that you may have discovered something. If you see a quick look to one family member or another, or if you notice another non-verbal sign, ask about it. Say, "Mom, I noticed a special look you gave Dad; what does that mean?"

With the prevalence of drugs, alcohol, child abuse (emotional, physical, and sexual), be aware of subtle signs of problems in these areas and always consider these as possibilities. If you get some clues or if you intuit a problem in these areas, carefully assess the situation. It is not a question of whether or not you are going to ask about your concerns, but rather of *when* and *how* you are going to ask the questions in order to ensure therapeutic gains for the family rather than to cause defensiveness or denials. Your main purpose is to benefit the family and the child. Questions to keep in mind are: "Do you have enough therapeutic maneuvers, motivational links, strategies, referral agencies, and auxiliary services to keep the family in a counseling relationship after this information has been brought into the open?" and "How can you bring the issue into the open in a way that will be therapeutically beneficial for the child?" If you seem to be getting the impression that something more is going on in this area, go slowly. Gather more information, and, if need be, be willing to move away from this intervention model into more of a consultant/referral agent to outside resources and agencies that are better equipped and have the expertise to deal with these complex problems on a longer-term basis.

After exploring the reasons for why the parents think the child is doing what he is doing, and after inquiring about possible related issues, you and the family are ready to move to Step Three.

(Incidentally, it is not always necessary or most expedient to go through the formal steps of the model in order.Once the structure of the model is well known, you can be more creative with the procedures to achieve the same results. However, from the onset you need to be aware that sometimes the model does not proceed as sequentially as you might like, so you need to be flexible. For example, you may be finishing Step Five and getting ready to end the session when the parents bring up the "real reason" they are having problems (the hidden agenda). Then you have to drop back and deal with that before you can go on. I believe that this second step is one of the most critical procedures of this model. If the counselor doesn't get to (and erode) the important beliefs, you can almost count on the later interventions not working. When the counselor discovers some of the important beliefs, she needs to be caring and non-blaming, and she must point out the *reasonableness* or *normality* of the various beliefs up until this point in time. The counselor's task at this important juncture is to help the family to find normality and reasonableness for their perspectives even though their adherence to these beliefs partially account for the child's current inappropriate behavior. One of the diagnostic, probing procedures that helps the counselor to understand the reasonable perspective from which the parents are coming is to explore the parents' family of origin for what systems therapists call "transgenerational" issues. Many times, parents' beliefs about why the child is behaving the way he is, or why they behave the way they do toward the child, stems from their family of origin, either in terms of their assimilation of their parents' values and beliefs, or their reactions against them. For example, in the previous book I related the case of a woman whose son was cussing her out (Chapter II, pp. 41-42). When I asked her if that was a problem and if she would like the behavior changed, she indicated that it was a problem but felt she couldn't change it. After I had explored this view with her she came up with several beliefs and excuses for letting the son continue to cuss her out (*e.g.,* she cussed, "What's good for the goose is good for the gander", "He should know better", and so forth). After eroding these beliefs as best I could, I asked about her parents and if she was allowed to cuss her mother out (transgenerational issues). At this point she indicated that her mother was crazy and would *never* let her express her true feelings. She indicated that she had made a vow: "If I ever had any kids, they would never have to be afraid to tell me what they truly felt or thought." After further exploring this transgenerational perspective with her, the *reasonableness* of why she had been bending over backward became very clear; in essence she was allowing the boy to express his "true feelings" toward her. In any event, if you can see—from an objective, non-blaming viewpoint—the reasonableness of where the parent is coming from, you can use that information to challenge the parent to act and communicate in a different way to help to solve the existing problem.

In this particular case, after pointing out the reasonableness of this woman's actions based on her own mother's treatment of her feelings and thoughts, I challenged her. Since the son's cussing was a problem to her, I asked her to see if she could set some limits, give her son a clear message to stop this inappropriate behavior in a way that was not "crazy" like her mother, and in a way that would enable her son to feel that he could still express his "feelings and thoughts" in a reasonable and appropriate way. This concept of transgenerational issues will be discussed further in Chapter Four.

Step Three: Past Attempted Solutions to the Problem

Step Three of the model involves exploring actions which the parents have already taken to get their child to do the goal behavior. Listen very carefully and take notes, if necessary, to record what was actually said and done to correct the problem. It is helpful to have the parents give you examples in the session. Say to the parents, "Show me. Give me an actual example of what you said to him." Then ask, "Did that work? What did you say and do when that did not work? What did you do to back it up? Did that work?" Make note of these examples, especially the actual language used so that you can refer to them later in the summary stage of the counseling session. Remember, to work this model effectively, you have to memorize the major categories of ineffective communication patterns in Chapter Three of *How to Deal with Discipline Problems in the Schools*. If the child is doing something inappropriate in the session, you can move from what the parents report that they do to "process" information and watch what the parents actually do and say. If the child talks back to the parents or is hyperactive in the sesson, see what the parents say or do about the behavior. Usually they ignore the behavior or use vague communication patterns which tell the child that it is okay to continue the behavior. If the parents ignore the inappropriate behavior and it is getting out of hand in the session, ask them if the student's behavior is bothering them. If so, ask them to correct it and watch what they say and do. Ask the parents if what is going on in the session is typical of what usually happens at home. The story of the junior-high-school boy who was not doing his homework, in *How to Deal with Discipline Problems in the Schools,* Chapter VI, pp. 115-116, illustrates this move to process information. The boy was acting out in the session. When the mother was asked if the boy's behavior bothered her, she indicated that it did. However, when she attempted to correct the boy's inappropriate behavior, she asked if he needed to go to the bathroom, giving him a ready-made excuse.

Another example of this paying attention to "process" information is in Chapter II, pp. 41-42. When the mother asked her son to tell her what he thought of her, he told her she was full of s____. In this situation the mother basically ignored the inappropriate behavior stating that she was glad he was sharing his true feelings in front of the counselor. By not taking any action to prevent the behavior in the session, she indicated how she handled problems at home. In fact, when asked about this later in the session, she indicated that she couldn't do anything about his cussing and had similar but worse problems with him at home. At home when he cussed, she tried to turn a deaf ear. If the "deaf ear" trick didn't work, she would leave the room, lock herself in her bedroom and wait until he calmed down. She was following the advice of one of the popular psychological methods of the day—which was to "avoid a power struggle". This is the same case I just mentioned in Step Two—"Analysis of Belief-Systems"—in which the reasonableness of the mother's not taking an active stand was in part related to the transgenerational issues of how her mother had treated her. The important point here is that through the analysis of "process" information enacted in front of your very eyes in the session, you can see how intricately related parents' beliefs, values, and family of origin are to what they say and do.

During this step of the model, you need to recognize vague, abstract, or indirect communication patterns that ultimately give the choice of behavior to the child. The implicit message of such communication is that the child really doesn't have to stop the inappropriate behavior unless he wants to. The parents, in essence, just hope that the child will want to do this on his own.

At this step of the model, you are just making note of the things which parents have actually tried in order to correct the problem. You are not necessarily pointing out to the parents how their indirect messages give the child a choice. Step Three primarily involves information-gathering and preparation for Step Five of the method. After you have explored and made note (using the parents' own language) of all the things the parents have attempted, you are ready to move to Step Four.

Step Four: *Previous Successes*

In Step Four you ask the parents to recall situations in which they have been successful in getting their child to do what they wanted even though the child did not want to do it. Again, take notes and ask the parents what they said and did to be successful. Have them give you actual examples. Some parents do not feel that they are successful in anything; others appear helpless. You may need to use creative questioning to help them see that they are successful in many areas. If the parents do not come up with some successes on their own, you can start with some of these standard inquiries to help them see how successful they really are:

Does he have chores that he has to do around the house that he doesn't like to do? How do you get him to do them?

Did he want to come to this counseling session? How did you get him to come?

When you say that he doesn't do anything until the tenth time, what do you say and do on the tenth time to be so successful?

Does he have to be in the house at certain times? How do you get him to do that?

Is he properly toilet-trained? How did you get him to do that? Did he initially want to do that?

When you say that you punish him (restrict him, spank him, send him to his room), how do you do that? Did he want to be on restriction for a month?

Does he have to go to church or family reunions when he doesn't want to?

Does he have any table manners? Does he eat with a fork and spoon? How did you get him to do that?

In these and similar inquiries, you are trying to draw out the fact that parents are successful and can make certain behaviors happen when they communicate clearly and specifically, and when they insist. When it is important enough to them to make it happen, they are very successful. By taking a clear stand on the issue, by giving specific, direct messages and then backing them up, they get their child to do what they want him to do even though he might have hated doing the required task.

When you ask parents to give you examples of successes, stress not only what parents *said,* but draw out what they *did,* especially if the child did not initially comply. In this way you will demonstrate that parental success was tied to clear, specific messages and specific behavioral actions which conveyed to the child that he had no choice in the matter, he was to do what was expected, and he was to do it right away. For example, question a mother who says that she can't get the kids to do anything until the tenth time.

Counselor: On the tenth time, when you are *successful,* what do you actually say and do?
Parent: Well, I finally get so mad at him, I tell him to take out the garbage right now, and I mean *right now.*
Counselor: Does he take out the garbage right then?
Parent: You're darn right he takes it out!

Whether the answer is "yes" or "no", the counselor needs to follow up with inquiries about what she did or about what she would have done if he hadn't complied.

Counselor: If he hadn't taken the garbage out, what would you have done?
Parent: I would have gone over there, taken him by the arm, and helped him get started right away.

Clear, direct messages convey to the child in specific terms what is to be done, and reflects an underlying adult attitude of authority and concern. This attitude reflects the following ideas:

(1) I'm willing to take over and be a parent in this situation and give some structure and guidance to ensure success;

(2) It is reasonable to expect and tell you, the child, to behave this way;

(3) I see you, the child, as capable of doing what is asked because I would not ask something of you that you couldn't do;

(4) and you will do what is requested without further discussion—you have no choice.

Remind parents that this is not an authoritarian, hostile dogmatic position of telling students when and where to jump, and how high. This method should be used only with specific, highly valued non-negotiable behaviors required for the child's well-being, and they should be framed within a context of love and caring. Try to help the parents realize that they are already successful parents in many areas and that their successes entailed believing that the child was capable; believing that they were reasonable in expecting him to behave; using clear, specific language; and backing up the message with appropriate behavioral interventions to make him do what was expected.

After you have helped the parents to see the many areas in which they are successful at getting their children to do what they want, as well as to see and understand how they have done so, you are ready to move to the next step.

Step Five: Summary

In Step Five, all the information comes together in a way that challenges the parents to solve the goal behavior (Step One) if they so desire. Again, you have to use all of your counseling skills to be caring, empathetic, and non-blaming, yet you must be clear and direct about what you see and understand to be happening. During this summary stage, you begin by reviewing Step Four of the model. Give some examples from your notes of what the parents said and did when they were successful, using their own words. You want to use the parents' own words because this technique helps to insure ownership and responsibility for the action taken. By reviewing this way, you underscore the principles used and help to ensure the parents' understanding. Point out in the areas where they have been successful that they took an active leadership role; they gave clear, specific, concrete directions; and they consistently and systematically backed them up so that the student had to do the desired behavior. There was no choice in the matter.

Stress that in the particular area of difficulty (Step One—reiterate the targeted goal behavior), they have been operating under completely different principles and communication patterns. By reviewing your notes on Step Three, reiterate what the parents have tried in order to get the child to be successful. Again, make sure that you use the *exact* language which they used. This is done so that the parents cannot deny what they have said. Point out that these attempts, even though they were not successful, were *reasonable* because they were based on erroneous beliefs that saw the child as incapable of doing what was wanted, or that saw a parental demand for the behavior as inappropriate. At this point, review the many parental beliefs given (Step Two—Analysis of Beliefs), and to prove the beliefs erroneous and no longer viable reasons for allowing the child to act inappropriately, give examples of contradictory evidence provided by the parents themselves. Commend the parents for trying; after all, they have tried all kinds of things (Step Three). However, point out that they have been using two completely different communication patterns and principles. When they have been unsuccessful, they have given vague, abstract, indirect, unclear messages, giving the child the choice of whether or not to comply, and have not backed up their expectations with behaviors that conveyed to the child that he had no choice in the matter. However, when they have been successful, they have communicated in clear, specific, direct terms; they were willing to lead and decide what the child was going to do; and they consistently backed up their demands with non-punishing behaviors that said, "There is no way out; you are going to do what is expected, and you will be successful." Point out that the ineffective communication and back-up techniques were reasonable, given their beliefs. Underscore, though, that those beliefs have now been dispelled or eroded through their own observable evidence of the child's competence. Thus the parents are now free, if they so desire, to use the same communication patterns and principles that have proven successful in other areas (Step Four) to have the child be successful in the goal behavior (Step One).

In most situations, the simple truth is that the parents have not told the student what to do, or they have not backed up their demand in a consistent fashion. In many cases, at this point of summarizing the process, the parents indicate that they understand what has happened and know what to do. Usually, the healthier the family is, and the more the child's problem really is just a school problem, the more effective the parents are in taking over and accomplishing quick results.

Many "normal" parents have been "psychologized" to the point of immobility, however. They want to do what is best for the child, but they don't know, or don't believe that they know, what to do. They're sure that they don't know enough and will cause great psychological harm to the child if they do the wrong thing. They are constantly bombarded with differing opinions on the latest causes and cures for inappropriate behavior. Many parents are looking for permission to be parents. They want to be told that it is okay to take an active stand and, if necessary, to make a reluctant student go to school and get at least straight C's. When parents who love their children and want the best for them feel that they have permission to exert legitimate parental control, and know what to do, they are usually amazed at the remarkable changes in their child's behavior. Their child will make a complete turn-around and feel good about it. After the parents take over and finally set reasonable limits, the student ultimately gains more freedom and flexibility, and earns the family's trust. When the student is successful, the parents have little to fight over, like him better, grow to trust him more, and see him as being more mature and responsible. Because of the student's new "maturity" and "responsibility" the parents give him more independence: they "get off his back" and let him make most of his own decisions.

Step Six: *Review of What the Parents Have Learned—An Optional Step*

This optional step is for parents that you sense are somewhat dysfunctional, have not fully understood the principles of the method, or who are rather authoritarian, hostile, or abusive. Under these circumstances, ask the parents to tell you in their own words what they learned from the counseling session. Listen carefully for any misinformation and help to clarify any misunderstood principles or messages.

For example, if a father says, "Yeah, I get the message—tell the kids what I want them to do, when I want them to do it, and if they don't do it the first time, let them have it, so they know I mean business." You might say, "No. That's not exactly what was said. What was said was.... Can you see how this is different?" Or you might bluntly ask the father if he really wants to beat his children and hurt them, or wouldn't he, if given a choice, rather develop a way to get them to do what he wanted them to do without having to beat them?

As another option, you can tell the father that when he punishes or beats his children, it is a variation of the "if 'x'/then 'y' " contract, which says to the child that it is okay for him to behave inappropriately as long as he is willing to be punished. Ask the father which message he would rather give:

(1) Do "x" (be successful), or "y", (be a failure). Either is okay with me; it is your choice. However, if you do "y", I am going to punish you; or

(2) Do "x". Be successful. There is no choice. I care about you and love you. I know that you can do it, and I'm willing to be a parent and help you in any way I can to ensure your success.

Bringing this understanding out into the open and discussing it forces the parents to clarify what they really want to do. You hope that this maneuver will build some therapeutic safeguards so that they will not hurt or abuse the child after they leave the session. In any case, you have made the choice clear:

(1) If you give a clear message for success and do everything in your power to make that happen without punishing or hurting your child, the message is that you love your child, care about him, and wish him to be successful.

(2) But if you beat your child after you have gone through this method, it is a clear message to the child and to others involved that you do not like your child, you really want to hurt him, and you want him to be unsuccessful.

Again, this may be another good place to explore transgenerational issues. Ask the father how his father treated him. How did he feel about it? How does he relate to his father now? Does he tell his father he loves him? Is this what he would want for his child? Is this the way he wants his child to talk and feel about him? Explore these issues to see if you can help the father to give clear messages of his intentions. Depending on the information that you get, you can reframe or relabel it in a more positive, benign way and use it to help to motivate the family to interact in a different way. More information on the relabeling process will be presented in Chapter Four.

Step Seven: *Enactment, Plan Ahead, or Role Play—Another Optional Step*

Occasionally, families say that they want the changes but are not sure that they can carry them out without some structure. At this point, you may have them plan what they will do and say if the child doesn't do the goal behavior. Suggest that they develop an individualized "lesson" plan similar to a teacher's lesson plan so that they can plan step by step what they will do. What will be their first step? What do they anticipate the child's response will be? How will they handle the response? Have the parents practice or role-play what they are going to say and do. If you do not like role-play or enactments, have them talk about their plans. Have them tell you what they plan to say and do. (See Appendix B: Parental Lesson Plan, and Appendix C: Helpful Hints for Parents.)

Give them some examples of what other parents have tried. If you know of techniques that other parents have used that can be helpful, relate them as suggestions. If they use such information successfully, then there is no problem, and you have saved a lot of time and energy. If they don't try any of the suggestions, or if they say that they tried them and they didn't work, this parental response in and of itself can then be used as a diagnostic probe. Their response should suggest to you that you either work longer with the family and intensify their interventions or that you start exploring other more complex and hidden dynamics or agendas that may be happening within the family. Remember to start with simple, straightforward interventions and thinking, and if they don't work, then move to more indirect and complex interventions that take into account more subtle family dynamics.

Have parents plan what they would do if the student intensifies the situation and tries to manipulate them by anger, crying, sulking, or fighting back. Help them to mobilize what back-up support-systems they might need in order to succeed, both in the home and in the school. You may need to enlist the teacher and/or principal, in-laws, neighbors, or other family members to help to coordinate proper back-up, follow-through, and consistency to ensure student success. In extreme situations, you may need to work with the police and court systems. Some families have even used police handcuffs, probation officers, or body-guards to make sure that truant, drug-taking, acting-out adolescents went to school, stayed there, and did what the parents expected until the student realized that the parents meant what they said and that he had no choice but to obey and to be successful.

You may wish to have the parents think about and plan for possible unforeseen consequences before they actually start their intervention plans. Ask how this might effect their relationship. Can their marriage stand the extra pressure of making this work? Can they do this together without getting angry at or blaming each other? Do they have the energy and persistence to make this happen, to follow through, and to be consistent 100% of the time even—if they are tired? Have they thought about what might happen if the student did become successful? How might that effect their relationship? Would they have anything else to talk about or to focus their energy on?

You might ask the parents to think over and talk about their plan before they actually start their intervention. If you feel that the parents really want to help their child acheive the goal behavior but may not follow through as consistently as you had hoped, you might force the situation by telling them in the presence of the child, "Make sure you are 100% committed before you start the intervention, because if you start it and then do not follow through, that tells your son that he can get away with it; that you don't love him; that you want him to be a failure; and, that you don't care about his education or his future well-being. So please don't start this unless you really are committed, because if you don't make it happen, that is a clear message to your son that you don't care."

This last maneuver, if used, puts the parents in a definite position of making up their minds as to what they value and what they are willing to do to make sure that their son is successful in school.

As you finish the session, give the parents materials that will help them to remember some of the general ideas expressed in the session. (A handout of helpful hints for parents can be found in Appendix C.) You might also suggest some further reading, such as *How to Get Your Children To Do What You Want Them To Do,* by Paul Wood, M.D., and Bernard Schuartz (Prentice Hall, 1978), and *Back in Control,* by Greg Bodenhammer (Prentice Hall, 1982).

After finishing the steps of the model, arrange a follow-up session. Usually, if the family functions well, you can set an appointment for a week or two later. However, indicate to the parents that they can call you anytime they like or that they can come in sooner if they are trying something and it doesn't seem to be working. Let them know that you prefer to have them call or come in immediately if they have any questions rather than wait a week or two and have the student continue to act inappropriately. In many situations where families are high functioning, issues can be settled in one session; in those situations, the success can be monitored by phone with the parents or through feedback reports from the teachers. In other situations, two or three sessions may be needed to help consult with the parents to see where things are breaking down. This may entail examining, or re-examining, belief-systems that were initially left out or were inadequately eroded, exploring transgenerational issues in greater detail, checking actual communication patterns, and, finally, checking on follow-through and consistency. Often in these latter cases, especially if the student has had a history of difficulties and manipulation of the parents, it is a question of supporting the parents and encouraging them enough to follow through until the student is convinced that they mean business and will not back down. Once the student gets the message, things start to change rather quickly.

In extreme cases, if the parents are working with you but have a very difficult child who is pushing the limits and testing the system, it may be necessary for you to help to coordinate some community and school resources to help the parents to be successful. For example, if you have a single mother with a sixteen-year-old son who is threatening her with physical abuse if she tries to make him go to school—you definitely need to get her some help. See if her ex-husband, other family members, neighbors, or church members can help. Have the mother hire a junior-college football-player or a body-guard. If necessary, get the police department, probation officers, or court system involved, especially if you have worked with them ahead of time and they know and support the program. As a last resort, if the school system is supportive and the district has worked out a plan to support teachers and parents in solving some of these problems, a support team backed by the district truant officer can be sent to the home to help the mother get the boy to school on time. If your counseling message to the parents is, "If it is important, then make it happen," then your message to the school, community, and legal system should be, "If education is important, then develop support systems to help parents and teachers make it happen."

Finally, if you get parents who are not going to work to solve the problem or whose value system actively supports the child's inappropriate behavior, clarify that fact in a non-blaming, non-judgmental way, but make it very explicit so that there can be no misunderstanding on the parents' or the child's part that the inappropriate behavior is what they want to happen and they are very successful at it. As an example of this, a psychiatrist told me about a case of professional thieves who had a son on drugs. The family was referred to him from probation because the boy was arrested for stealing while he was under the influence of drugs. After going through family counseling, the family was very successful at getting the child off drugs (the parents' goal), but when asked about stopping the boy from stealing, they weren't interested. They had had three to four generations of professional thieves in their family, and they could see no reason to stop the tradition. However, it was pointed out to them how successful they really were as parents, even though it was in direct contrast to our society's point of view.

You now have a brief overview of the seven steps of the family counseling model. In the next few chapters, more of the important issues, concepts, and ideas that typically come up in counseling sessions will be explored to help you better understand the philosophy, methods, and techniques of this approach.

Chapter IV: Other Helpful Concepts, Ideas, and Belief-Systems

This chapter will be a potpourri of concepts, ideas, and belief-systems that the counselor or school psychologist will find helpful in working with this model. The intent of this chapter is to expand on the basic framework and knowledge which you already have and explore some of the variations that might arise.

Beliefs

In my first book on this model, we covered some of the major beliefs which parents and teachers use, and some typical ways of trying to erode them. Here are a few other beliefs that occasionally emerge in family sessions.

A. *Against the Child's True Nature*

Some parents and teachers believe that children have a "true nature" and that to try to correct behavior that is inherently "natural" violates natural law. For example, some—and I would like to emphasize *some*—Montessori schools believe that children need to get up, move around, experience everything, and express themselves. The Montessori philosophy, as translated by some overzealous teachers and parents, sees alternative styles of teaching as not being in the best interests of the student and going against his "true nature". A. S. Neil, the author of *Summerhill,* a popular book in the 60's, is another proponent of this type of belief. He started a school in which the child was able to go back to his "true nature"; that is, he could express himself, and behave as he liked, without the constraints of society or social custom. The belief was that if the adult allowed the child to be "free", then the child would naturally grow and develop. With this freedom to experience his true nature, the child would naturally become a self-motivated, caring individual and would intrinsically learn and choose to make appropriate decisions. Some popular child-rearing methods based on certain popular psychological theories have advocated that the child has rights; that he needs to express himself, get in touch with his feelings, grow to his full potential, and achieve self-actualization. Again, the belief is that if the child is encouraged to be inner-directed, in touch with his feelings and free to express himself, he will become a genuine, caring, spontaneous, creative, self-directed, and free human being. Some parents and teachers fervently believe in the Montessori, Summerhill, or other similar approaches, and they see any efforts to discipline, control, guide, restrict or set limits as bad, evil, or contrary to the student's true nature. Some people also tie this philosophy into the child's creativity. They feel that the child needs to be "spontaneous" and "free" to be creative and that any effort to discipline or control this spontaneity stifles the creative process. Although there are degrees of truth in these particular perspectives, extreme freedom, as well as extreme control, often lead to negative and unforeseen consequences. I advocate taking a moderate position—that is, integrating freedom and control to obtain the best results.

However, regardless of what my personal beliefs are, or what yours are, in questioning parents who believe that control stifles creativity or the child's "true nature", ask simple questions, such as, "How is having a student be quiet while the teacher is giving instructions stifling the student's creativity?" "Is it beyond the student's nature and capabilities to sit still for two minutes while the teacher is giving instructions so all the children can get the information before starting their projects? Their creative endeavors?" "If the student behaves appropriately, how does that stifle his intellectual or academic creativity?" "What evidence do you have that your child's creativity is being stifled?" "Have you ever known any students who act appropriately and yet are creative? How do you account for those students who act appropriately and are creative, both academically and artistically?"

Again, although there might be some element of truth in these beliefs, come back to the question of whether the belief has any relevance to the specific behavior in question. Is the behavior appropriate for the time and place? What leads the parents to believe that the child cannot or should not do the behavior in this particular time and place? When people have these beliefs, the question is, is the child's "true nature" really reflected in the specific behavior under question?

B. *Bill of Rights, Children's Rights, and Freedom of Expression*

Another belief-system perceives classroom discipline as an unwarranted limitation on freedom of expression, and in some cases, as "unconstitutional". Some parents tell teachers that they don't want their kids to become robots, they don't want them to become automatons who perform without thinking. They don't want the teachers to have so much authority and power that they become dictators. The parents want their children to stand up for themselves, be more independent, and make their own decisions rather than "blindly" conforming to the rules.

The first thing to point out to these parents is how very successful they are, and how they've gotten their child to do exactly what they wanted him to; the child is standing up for himself, is standing up to the teacher, and he is not following the school rules. The question is, is that okay with the parents? Do they prefer to have their child continue to act inappropriately from the school's perspective, even if he gets straight F's, which in all probability will ultimately reduce his freedom of choice, especially if he doesn't learn how to read or write?

Some parents really get locked into the idea that control goes against the child's rights; they feel that it tends to make the child dependent, a follower, and a person who is unable to express himself. When you hear this position, ask, "How is this particular form of control (*e.g.,* raising his hand before speaking out) going to make him dependent or prevent him from expressing himself?" "How is it going against his nature or rights?" "How is sitting down and doing his math work tied in to his loss of creativity or his freedom?" Have the parent explain his or her position and beliefs to the child, the school, and to you so everyone will at least know what the rules of the game are. Check for transgenerational issues so that you can get a better understanding of how the parents' own upbringing is influencing their present beliefs. (Transgenerational issues will be explored and explained later in this chapter.) Have the parents clarify what is wanted or expected of the child in specfic behavioral terms. Then the parents can judge how successful they have been at getting the student to act in accordance with the belief.

I had a well-educated, upper-middle-class father tell me that his six-year-old son told him "to go f⎯⎯ off". When I asked the father if that was a problem to him, and if he would like to change that behavior, he told me it was "no problem". He wanted his son to be able to freely express himself, not have to be afraid of him or have to repress his true feelings. He felt that children have rights too; they are individuals who have the right to say what they think and feel. The way I look at this is, "There is no problem until there is a problem." Luckily, I don't have to live with this youngster for the next fifteen years. The point is, the father is very successful at getting the son to do what he wants—the son is "truly" expressing himself.

C. *Out of Sight, Out of Mind*

Another popular belief-system which parents have is that they can't control their child when he's out of their sight. This message has been given many times to students. Since the students in school are out of the parents' sight, the school bears responsibility for the child's inappropriate behavior. The question to ask the parents is, "What leads you to believe that you cannot control your child when he is out of your sight?"

Since this message has been transmitted to the child, ask the parents, "Well, that's a clear message to your child that anytime you're not around he can do anything he wants. Is that all right with you, or would you like to change that?" Or you might say, "Since he knows that you don't believe you are capable of controlling him when he is out of your sight, then that means when you are gone he can do whatever he wants to. Is this okay with you? By the way, when you are gone, does he take drugs, steal, exceed the speed limit, or have wild sex orgies without your setting some rules and taking some active steps to stop him?"

Challenge the parents on their belief that they can't control him when he is out of their sight. Point out the inconsistencies and question them.

Counselor:	Tell me, does your son have a curfew?
Parent:	Oh yes, he has to be in by 9:00 on weekdays and 12:00 on weekends.
Counselor:	Does he come home?
Parent:	Yes. I tell him he has to be in by 12:00.
Counselor:	He was out of your sight and yet he came home. How did you get him to come home?
Parent:	Well, he just knew what the rules were and that he had to come home.
Counselor:	Okay, so you're very successful even though you're out of his sight. You told him he had to be home, he knew the rules, and he followed them. But in this area of going to school and acting appropriately he has gotten a different message. You basically have said, "I have no control in this area. I don't expect you to behave." And he hasn't. Is that a problem to you, and would you like to change the message that you're giving to your son? Because I'm absolutely sure that if you give him a new set of rules and tell him that while he is in school he must do what the teacher says, he will.

An interesting example of this "out-of-sight" belief was given to me by a teacher in a weekend University extension class. She started the conversation by stating that she and her son were having some minor problems at school. Simple issues had escalated into inappropriate and even dangerous behavior: her son was now scratching and biting other children. Supposedly, he was a very creative youngster who finished his work quickly and would then run around the room doing whatever he wanted. She said her initial concern was that the school was not taking enough of an active stance to prevent the behavior. She stated later that the school personnel confided that her son's behavior was okay as long as he completed his work.

Her story had a lot of inconsistencies and she seemed somewhat proud of the fact that her child was acting up. Since this was the very end of the class meeting and not a counseling session, I quickly explored with her some possibilities and tied them into the class material presented.

I suggested that she make sure she was giving a clear message to her son about his inappropriate behavior. I also suggested that she develop some back-up techniques in the event that giving a clear message did not work. In addition, I encouraged her to take an active stance to stop the behavior, even if the school did not see it as a problem. As the parent, she should tell the school that this behavior was inappropriate from her perspective and that she was going to do whatever she needed to do to stop the behavior; furthermore, let them know that she would like their cooperation in preventing this behavior in the classroom.

As we talked, she indicated that the extension class had prompted her to analyze all her belief-systems that might account for the problems she was having with her son. Since the boy and his father weren't present, it was difficult to go into great detail with her. I casually mentioned one particular belief that I hadn't covered in the seminar: "One of the things some people believe," I told her, "is that they can't control their kids when they're out of sight." With that, her face lit up, "That's it! That's the one. That's what is happening. I don't trust him out of my sight, and I don't believe he will behave appropriately when I'm not there." She began to give example after example.

I told her that she should explore this belief, challenge it, and discover its origin.

She indicated that her lack of trust was such that when she sent her son to his room she'd say, "I can't even trust you in your room by yourself. I don't trust you alone long enough to take your punishment." She would then go into his room to observe him taking his punishment. In terms of communications theory, this action gives a clear message to the son—she doesn't really trust him. He knows that when she's out of sight he doesn't have to act appropriately because no one expects him to. Therefore, it's okay for him to act inappropriately.

Be aware of this belief, and be prepared to question and challenge the parent who holds it. Remember, always look for the *evidence* to erode these types of beliefs. Keep in mind that beliefs, such as this one, might sometimes reflect more important, hidden beliefs such as "the boy can't be trusted out of sight because he is just like his good-for-nothing father." It may also reflect the fact that the mother herself feels untrustworthy. The belief may be a carryover from her own youth when she couldn't be trusted. The belief also may have philosophical, religious, or sexually related overtones (*e.g.*, original sin, the basic inherent untrustworthiness of people, all males are alike, and so forth). The question to keep in mind is, "Why do you believe that he can't be trusted, and how did he get that way?" If you sense any of these hidden issues, bring them up and question them; check out transgenerational issues; bring them out into the open and erode them.

D. *Beliefs about Discipline*

Under this category of beliefs, counselors have to be aware of at least two possible extremes. At one extreme is an apparent lack of discipline; at the other is an apparent excess of discipline, punishment, and/or abuse. The first situation may be owing to a lack of parental skills, concern, or involvement. An apparent lack of discipline could also be a reasonable reaction and conscious choice made by the parent to *not* discipline because of previous negative personal life experiences with discipline in the home or in school. Some adults were traumatized by harsh disciplinary actions taken by their parents or by someone in the school system. Most of us remember an incident during our education when a teacher ridiculed or embarrassed another student and/or physically punished a student with extreme measures. Some of these students, after becoming parents, do not trust the school; they either openly do not support the school's effort to discipline their children, or they will say what you want to hear but then won't follow through or support your efforts to stop the student's inappropriate behavior. This position is a reaction to negative, authoritarian, hostile, and abusive parenting or teaching.

If it appears that a lack of parental skills is the problem, work with the parents and teach them. If the problem seems to be a lack of concern and involvement, use whatever methods are necessary to get the parents to take a stand and get involved. Check for transgenerational issues, but basically push the parents to take a stand: Are they going to get involved or not? If this approach fails, and the parents indicate they are not willing to get involved, put pressure on them by having the school file for child neglect and by getting various community agencies involved.

If the parents have made a conscious choice to not discipline, explore the parents' beliefs, transgenerational issues, and trans-school issues to challenge them to take a different perspective. Let them see that their perspective is reasonable, given their life experiences, but also point out how their "reasonableness" has led to unfortunate consequences. Ask them what they really want for their child. Ask if they want their child to flunk out of school, be truant, get into trouble, talk back to the teacher and disrupt the classroom. Ask them, too, if they would be willing to work with the school to take appropriate actions to stop these behaviors; however, ask them if they can do so in such a way that the process doesn't revive or parallel their own previous negative life experiences. By questioning them in this manner, your hope is to help them realize the issues involved, and as a result, to take a stand to stop the inappropriate behavior.

Parents who grew up with harsh discipline typically develop one of two styles. Either they react to the harsh discipline and decide not to act in the same way toward their children, or they say, "I was raised that way, and it didn't hurt me. Since I turned out okay, the same kind of discipline is okay for my children." Questioning-techniques and examples for this first position have been presented. The last position, in some ways, is harder to deal with, especially if parents add religious beliefs such as, "Spare the rod, spoil the child". If this latter position is the case, stay with the transgenerational issues as much as possible and have the parents focus on some of their early impressions, fears, thoughts, or feelings toward their parent's harsh treatment. Ask, "Did you like it?" "Do you like your parents now?" "Is the way you currently relate to, think, and feel about your parents the way you want things to turn out between you and your children?" Ask questions to get at their intents, hopes, and wishes for their children, and then see if they can be convinced of a better way to reach their goal without beating their child or using harsh treatment. After exploring these issues, ask the parents in front of the child, "If you had a choice and you could get your son to do what you wanted him to without having to beat him, would you prefer to do that, or would you like to continue to beat him?"

E. *Over-Compensation*

A common belief of special-education teachers and parents with children in special-education programs is that their

Other Helpful Concepts, Ideas, and Belief-Systems   87

children tire out from expending so much time and energy on a task. They say that it takes so much energy on the child's part to concentrate, or that the child compensates so well, that they can't expect the child to stay on task as long as do "normal" children. While it might in fact be harder for a particular student to stay on task, the longer he stays on task and learns the skills he needs, the easier it will be to stay on task in the future. Without being completely unreasonable, have the student stay on task just as everyone else does. (Helen Keller did not want to stay on task when doing her homework and school assignments. Initially, it was difficult for Keller to stay on task and for her teacher to make her stay on task. I am sure that it took more time, energy, compensation, and concentration on Keller's part than it would have for "normal" children to master the same tasks. Yet, I am equally sure that after spending more time doing the various tasks and mastering the basic skills, it became relatively easier to do these tasks—and to do them considerably better.)

The whole area of attentional deficit disorder (A.D.D.), lack of attention and concentration, and lack of energy necessary to compensate for the apparent deficits is, I think, fraught with misinformation, misconceptions, and myths. I have seen children who supposedly had A.D.D. pay attention and do the most amazing tasks when the tasks were highly structured, challenging, and properly taught. These students, just as would "normal" students, would go through initial periods of frustration and concerted effort to master a new task, but, after mastery, the amount of time and energy required to accomplish the task was substantially reduced.

If the initial information and data from the McInnis Assured Readiness for Learning Program can be substantiated, then most of the primary and secondary effects and symptoms of what we currently call A.D.D. will be eliminated. Dr. McInnis has indicated that in the past seven years as a school psychologist in the public schools, he placed only one child in special education—and she was mentally retarded. All other children who were diagnosed or assumed to be hyperactive or have A.D.D. were helped by his program and kept in regular classes as "normal", productive, skilled children.

Remember, feel for the children, be sensitive to their needs, but love them enough to give them structure; teach them to concentrate better, become more effective and efficient, *and* learn.

F. *Inner Ear Imbalance and Failure of the Body to Appropriately Filter Medication*

Practitioners frequently tell me about cases which they have had in which parents have been told by doctors that the child's learning- and behavior-problems are related to inner ear imbalance. When the medications don't seem to improve the condition, the fault lies in the body's filtering system for that particular medication, which is not working properly. Here again, I always say, if the evidence is there, believe it; do whatever is necessary and congruent with that particular belief to solve the problem. There are possible elements of truth and effectiveness in the hundreds of cures that I have heard over the years for learning- and behavior-difficulties. When I am in doubt, however, I always fall back on "show me the evidence". Does the behavior happen under certain conditions? Does the behavior stop when someone takes an active stand and tells the child to stop the specific behavior? Does the child have the same learning- and behavior-problems in all seven classes? If someone offered the child $1,000 to stop doing the inappropriate behavior and start doing what they wanted him to, could he do it? If so, then perhaps he has more control than we initially gave him credit for. Some belief-systems become very complex and sophisticated, and the technical aspects are definitely beyond our scope of training and expertise.

At times like these, you don't want to be ignorant and say and do things that might be harmful. Take your time. Ask a lot of questions. Gather information. Talk to the experts; have them explain their ideas and how they work. Have an open mind and explore all possibilities, but, at the same time be a little bit skeptical and really question and explore in concrete, specific ways the experts' reasoning on how this given process works with regard to the specific problem. For example, I would love to know, given this belief about inner ear imbalance, if a student with certain learning- and behavior-problems has the same difficulties when under different educational or social environments. If so, I would like to know how the experts explain the differences. If the filtering system does not work but I can walk up to a high-school student and give him

$1,000.00 to raise his hand and wait to be called on before he talks, to sit and act appropriately in class (however that appropriateness may be defined by the teacher), and to do his work and turn it in on time for that one period, and he can do it—how would they explain that phenomenon?

G. *Tourette Syndrome*

Always look for the evidence to substantiate a particular belief, no matter what the belief. Again, I have had practitioners ask me what I think of the current popular diagnosis of Tourette Syndrome. I say the same thing I say about hyperactivity, inner ear imbalance, or brain damage: If you have overwhelming evidence confirming the diagnosis then the student *has* a problem. Do whatever is necessary and congruent with that belief-system to solve the problem. If you have contradictory evidence that suggests that the student can control himself, then he probably doesn't have that particular problem.

I assume that there is such a thing as Tourette Syndrome. However, I am sure that it is a fairly rare phenomenon. What I am concerned about is that the diagnosis has become so popular that some people are using it as an acceptable excuse for inappropriate behavior, just as A.D.D. and hyperactivity have become. The incidence of all three of these "conditions" has increased over the past few years, and I'm sure (this is tongue-in-cheek) that there must be some type of newly discovered but common genetic basis.

As a first step in questioning the belief that the child's problems are being caused by Tourette Syndrome, I would look for all the evidence to either support or challenge that contention. I would use such questions as: Does the student stop cussing and acting inappropriately when the principal walks in? During certain periods of the day if he was told to stop cussing? I was telling this to a group of school psychologists in Illinois when one of them said he had a case which perfectly illustrated this point. He stated that in the high school in which he worked, a "conservative, hard-nosed" teacher who would not put up with this type of behavior in his classroom told a student to "knock it off and never cuss again in my classroom". The school psychologist said the student never did cuss again in this particular teacher's classroom. However, he continued to have periodic episodes in his other classes. Presented with evidence such as this, even though I know experts say that Tourette kids are capable of controlling their impulses for short periods of time, it is hard to believe that the student has no control and can't learn to control himself better.

Language of Inference

Counselors need to keep their intuitive senses awake to the uses of language. When you listen to families talk, get a sense for the feeling or mood of the family. When the family uses certain words, or describes certain ideas or issues, allow yourself to take the language or ideas at least one step further and test the limits a little. At a deeper, more dynamic level, use this concept of "language of inference" to allow yourself to make some quantum leaps into the unknown and take a guess as to what the language suggests. When you do this, make the ideas your own; don't ask the parents if the thoughts are their's. For example, you might say something like this: "As I listen to all of this, I believe that if what you say were true, it might mean.... What do you think?" Don't say, "Are you thinking....?"

If you present the thoughts as your own, the parents will be able to react to "your crazy ideas and feelings". This clinical technique should be done with discretion in the school setting. This is more of an in-depth dynamic probe, and, depending on the nature of the problem and the dysfunction of the family, may open up the family more than you or they would like. You have to weigh the therapeutic importance of this technique against the limited time and scope available in the school setting. Carl Whitaker is a master of "language of inference". I refer you to the *Evolution of Psychotherapy* tapes ("The Blind Date Family Interview") or *From Psyche to Systems* by Neil (1975) for more-complete discussions of this concept. (See Appendix A.)

On a less sophisticated basis, I usually use the concept to infer that the language someone is using to describe one situation is a double message or symbolic for another situation. For example, if a father describes his daughter in negative ways ("She never listens to me." "She's a slob." "She has really let herself go." "I'm almost ashamed to be in public with her" and so forth.), I sometimes infer that the message is not just for the daughter, but for the mother as well. I try to be aware of the possibilities, but I usually do not bring them directly out in the open. If the father says, "She does...," and it is not clear who he is talking about, I will usually say something like, "She? Meaning your daughter?" Or "Do you mean *Sally* here is...?" It is hoped that this approach forces the father to separate the double message and send a clear single message to his daughter. This method makes the daughter's problem more concrete, specific, and easily defined. The definition of the daughter's problem in concrete terms enables me to work with the family to solve a real, tangible problem *vs.* an abstract, symbolic, or metaphoric one.

Family Life Cycle

One useful way to conceptualize a family system is to study it longitudinally along its time dimensions, life, or developmental stages. Frequently, family behavior-patterns, or, perhaps, family crises, become more understandable when seen within the context of the cycle or stage of development the family is in.

From a family life-cycle perspective, each intact family goes through more or less the same processes over time, passing through the same sequences or phases, each usually marked by a critical transition-point: marriage, birth of the first child, first child going to school, last child going to school, first or last adolescent leaving home, and so on. Much like an individual, a family can be viewed as going through a life-cycle.

From a family-systems perspective, psychiatric or behavioral symptoms appear in a family member when there is a break in the natural unfolding of the family life-cycle. The symptom can then be seen as a signal that the family is having problems mastering the tasks inherent in that stage of the life-cycle.

In counseling a family in the school setting, it is helpful to be aware of these major steps or life stages in a family's development so that as you gather information about the family, you can in turn use the information to better understand where the family is and what you might do to help them.

You can point out how other families have gone through these various stages, emphasizing the "normality" of such a process, even though you know and understand that doing so is difficult and perhaps stressful to them at the present time. You can also point out that in the adolescent stages, for instance, there is a major shift in roles and relationships. The child is moving from a complementary relationship with his parents in which the parents were in control in most situations, to a more symmetrical relationship where there is a greater degree of equality and independence between parents and children. This shift requires a new set of game rules and social skills that need to be worked out. You can then reframe some of the "trouble" as "confusion" over the rules, a lack of mastery of new skills, and normal "trial and error".

As a family counselor, you should become familiar with the major developmental tasks that need to be mastered at different stages of family life as well as some of the typical problems that emerge at those times. You can then develop some "planned spontaneous" reframing, relabeling, and questioning techniques, as well as suggestions and interventions for the family. In addition, the development of school-based family education programs can be very helpful in dealing with typical, non-dysfunctional family-growth and life-cycle issues.

During the "analysis of belief-systems" (Step Two in the model), if you feel that it is appropriate, bring up some of the more typical issues that arise at the different stages of the family life-cycle. Ask the parents if they feel that any of these issues might have some bearing on the student's difficulty at school. If the parents do feel that some of these issues might be involved, you can then try to erode them as best you can or talk about the "normal process" of that stage along with some of the tasks and skills that need to be worked on. Although you are not doing marriage therapy, sometimes questions regarding the implications of the student's behavior at various life-cycle stages with regard to the marriage relationship might be helpful. For example, if a senior in high school is the last child in the family and is getting ready to leave the home ("last-child-out-of-the-family", or "empty-nest", syndrome), it might be appropriate to explore with the family, in a general way, such issues as: "Have you thought about the advantages and disadvantages of having your son gone?" "How do you

Other Helpful Concepts, Ideas, and Belief-Systems

think his leaving will effect your marriage, both positively and negatively?" "Mom and Dad, what have you been planning on doing together when your son is gone?" Remember, in terms of this short term school approach, even if you talk about these issues, do not let parents use them as excuses for letting the child fail.

Process Information

"Process information" refers to an examination of what the parents are actually *doing* right there in the session to stop inappropriate behavior *vs.* what they say they do. To illustrate this concept, I would like to recall a previous case in which a junior-high-school boy was acting-out during the session (*How to Deal with Difficult Discipline Problems: A Family-Systems Approach, Chapter III, pg. 67; How To Deal With Discipline Problems,* Chapter VI, pp. 115-116). The single-parent mother was ignoring the behavior while trying to talk to me over the noise and distraction (Process information—she ignores the behavior.). The child's behavior kept escalating, and the mother continued to ignore it until I could no longer take it. Finally, I asked the mother if her son's present behavior bothered her. She strongly indicated that it was "bugging" her. At that point, I asked her if there was anything which she would like to say to her son about his behavior, to which she promptly said to him, "If you have to go to the bathroom, tell me." (Process information—unclear communication attempt to stop inappropriate behavior.) In this situation, it is very apparent that what the mother said to stop the child's inappropriate behavior—"If you have to go to the bathroom, tell me"—was not a clear, direct message to stop the inappropriate behavior. When the "process information" (what the mother actually says and does in the session *vs.* what she claims that she says and does) is right in front of you, use that information to help to illustrate the points you are trying to get across to the parents (effective *vs.* ineffective intervention and communication-patterns).

Normalization

The process of "normalization" attempts to bring some order and structure to a family, to give the family some context to understand the "normal process" they are going through. The process allows the family to gain some control and understanding of what is going on within the family and then to institute some positive changes. It is an attempt to stabilize some of the family energy and get it focused in a direction that will foster change in a positive direction. In a sense, "normalization" could be seen as a relabeling or reframing of the family's reality. The normalization process might entail using many of the "tricks of the trade", such as relabeling, reframing, describing the stage of the family lifecycle that the family is in, or pointing out the reasonableness of a particular belief-system based in part on life experiences or transgenerational issues. All of these techniques assist the family in seeing the "normal" process and pressures that they are going through.

As a counselor, you try to reduce some of the family's fears of being crazy and help them stop labeling, blaming, or interpreting each other's motives in negative, pathological, or hurtful ways. A characteristic which seems to be common in families in difficulty, especially those under a lot of stress, is that they tend to blame each other and interpret each other's motives in rather negative ways. As a counselor, you have to try to establish some degree of composure within the family, and, by building a "normalized" family context, help them to get past the blaming or negative labeling of each other and have them get on with the normal business of solving life's problems. In this process of normalizing family interactions, having the family members see their interactions from a different perspective or reframed in a different contextual reality, can be an opportunity for the family to grow and develop.

This "normalization" process is also a way for me to remind myself to see the individuals, and the family as a whole, in a more positive way, rather than in my professionally trained way of seeing pathology in most everything.

Kick-and-Support

At times it may become necessary to confront the parents and tell them exactly "how it is". To get the parent's attention may require stating the situation in blunt terms. (See Chapter 9, "Intensity" in Minuchin's *Family Therapy Techniques*.) What I call "kick-and-support" techniques entail direct confrontation with the parents to get them to see the reality of a situation; however, it is followed up with support, encouragement, and understanding for the reasonableness of their previous actions. This method clearly indicates to the parents that they must take a stand to make things better. This technique is similar in principle to the old behavioral cliche "disapprove of the behavior, not the child". In a sense, "kick" the parents (disapprove of the behavior), but strongly "support" them.

As an example of this technique, I will return to the case of the sixteen-year-old boy who told his mother she was full of s____ during a session. (*How To Deal With Discipline Problems in the Schools,* Chapter II, pp. 41-42.) Several nights after our session, and after the mother finally decided to take a stand and stop many of her son's inappropriate behaviors, she called me in a rather melancholy and philosophical mood. The mother, a well-educated professional, stated that since the session she had been doing a lot of thinking. She indicated that although she had changed a lot in her approach toward her son and that her new methods seemed to be working, she was starting to question herself. She said that in all honesty, after reviewing her life, the divorce, and her very busy life as a professional, she felt inadequate and "crummy" as a mother; in fact, she was not sure that she was a "good" parent. At this point, over the telephone, I used my "kick-and-support" technique.

Counselor: Right now, I don't care whether or not you are an inadequate, "crummy" mother. All I want to know is do you want your child to tell you that you are full of s____ ?
Parent: No.
Counselor: Do you know any mothers that are worse than you are?
Parent: Yes.
Counselor: Do they let their children swear at them?
Parent: No.
Counselor: Look, I don't know about you, but most parents whom I know, including myself, try to be the best parents we can. I also know in my heart of hearts that I fall short of what I would like to be as a parent to my kids. We all try. We all feel inadequate at times. But I don't care how inadequate any of us is, it doesn't give a child the right to say you are full of s____. If a child doesn't like something, he can talk to you about

	it in a more appropriate way. My parents were pretty good parents, but they could have done a lot better. At times during my adolescence, I didn't like some of the things that they did or that they made me do, but I'll tell you one thing: I *never* would have told them they were full of s____.
Parent:	I get the point.
Counselor:	Great. Kids may not like what you do as a parent, but they can learn to express themselves in a reasonable manner. By the way, if you think that you are that ineffective as a parent, you can see me in private practice, and I will charge you $75.00 an hour, twice a week for a year, and teach you parent-effectiveness and communication skills and....
Parent:	No, thanks. I get the point. I'm sure I can handle it.... (We continue to talk, and I support her and the interventions that she started with her son.)

"Kick" the parents and let them know there is no excuse for crazy, bizarre, inappropriate behavior—but "support" them. Let them know that parenting is sometimes tough, that you understand, that we all are human, that none of us is perfect, but that we do the best that we possibly can. Let parents know that you have to be a parent to raise your children; however, you do not have to be a *perfect* parent to raise your children.

Seating Arrangements

Watch how families arrange themselves when they sit down. Sometimes the arrangement can give you a tentative hunch or concept of possible family sub-system alignments or coalitions; it can give you an idea of who is close to whom, and who is distant. Be careful that your chairs and room arrangement don't force family members into an odd or unusual seating arrangement. If your room is set in such a way that there are enough seats with no obstacles or barriers between them, then as the family enters each member can choose where he or she would "naturally" wish to sit. Watch, and develop tentative hypotheses; gather more information to help give a contextual or face validity to your hunches. Use good sense and don't read too much into this analysis. Recognize, though, that sometimes a tremendous amount of information relating to the family can be gained from observing the order taken in the seating arrangements.

In one session, a family of four came into the room. Each member picked up a chair and moved it about four feet away from every other family member, each choosing to sit in separate corners of the room. After moving my chair so I could at least get a glimpse of everyone in the room without having to move around too much, I asked, "Well, what seems to be the problem?" A few moments passed before the father finally said, "I think we have a basic communication problem."

In another session, the family moved the chairs over to a table in the room. The father sat on one side of the table, and the mother and the children sat on the other side.

The husband and wife of another family came in and initially sat together. The child picked up his chair and tried to move it in between the husband and wife. When the father told him to sit on the other side, the boy threw a temper tantrum, and the mother then moved her chair over to let the boy sit between them.

Be aware of the seating arrangements and watch for "process information" on how the parents solve these in-session problems. Note the actual words and actions taken by the parent to correct the problem, and use this information later in the formal steps of the counseling model to help the parents compare and contrast their effective communication patterns with those that were ineffective.

Non-Verbal Interactions

This particular brief family-counseling approach generally does not pay any direct attention to non-verbal interactions. The non-verbal interactions are normally not drawn out into the open, not made an issue of, and not used to help uncover other feelings or meanings. Rarely do I draw attention to non-verbal interactions or ask for feelings about them. As a general rule I stay with a cognitive solution to the problem.

I divide non-verbal communication into two basic categories. In the first category the non-verbal communications are either designed to manipulate the parents away from the solution to the problem, or they are reactions to feelings created because of a lack of resolution of the family's problems.

When I encounter manipulative non-verbal interactions, I essentially ignore them and stay focused on a solution to the problem. When the non-verbal communications are caused by a lack of resolution, I find that if the problem is solved, most of these non-verbal innuendoes drop off and disappear; therefore, I see no reason to bring them up or ask people how they feel about them. People's feelings change after the problems are solved. In the second category, the information gained from observing reactive non-verbal interactions can be used by the counselor to help to qualify, clarify, or modify the original message. In this case, the information can be used to help to focus on and make clear the real issues and problems.

Even though you might not directly acknowledge those non-verbal communications, indirectly make mental note of them and be prepared to use some of that information to help to clarify or confirm some of your hunches or hypotheses of what might be going on in the family. By carefully observing the family members' non-verbal communication, you may get some ideas or leads that will allow you to follow up with some pointed questions. Again, these questions you would treat as your own, and you would ask them in such a way that no individual family member would be put on the spot. For example, if I get a sense from one family member's non-verbal communication that he or she does not agree with another member's point of view, I wouldn't say, "John, it seems like you disagree with your mom's perspective. How do you feel about what she has just said?" What I might say in this type of situation is, "You know, Mrs. Smith, if I was in your family and you said..., I might be wondering or thinking..., Is what you're trying to say more like..., or is it more like...?" (Put in your hunches or ideas with the intent that doing so will help the parents to clarify what they really want to say or have happen.) "If this is the case, how can the two of you work together as a team to resolve the problem?" (The intent here is to put the parents in charge and to make clear what needs to be done; it is not just a reaction to the non-verbal responses or to ask how people feel about them.)

There is nothing inherently wrong with working directly with non-verbal communication and trying to get at some of the deeper feelings of the family. However, with this short-term counseling approach designed to work in the school setting, it is best to remain more objective, to work indirectly with the non-verbal interactions, to put the parents in charge and to clarify what needs to be done, and to stay focused on the cognitive components of the problem and the solution to the problem. Your objective is to work quickly for an intervention and solution to that problem.

Symptoms Masking Other Problems

One of the tenets of most family-therapy approaches is that the identified patient (the IP) and his symptoms are a reflection of or serve a broader purpose in the family context. In most dysfunctional families, this tenet is probably the case. (See Cloe Madanes's *Strategic Family Therapy* and Jay Haley's *Leaving Home, Problem Solving Therapy,* and *Ordeal Therapy*.) However, many times, especially in typical school-related academic and behavioral problems, the symptom is just the symptom, the behavior is just the behavior. In most typical school-setting cases, you're not dealing with major dysfunctional families. The fact that the student is missing school is, sometimes, all that you need to deal with. If that behavior is stopped, then you have done your job. You do not have to do in-depth psychotherapy if a simple intervention works. Remember, you're in a school setting, not in private practice, and you have maybe one or two sessions at most.

When a student presents a symptom within the school setting, I usually explore three possibilities: (1) the symptom is just the symptom or problem; (2) the symptom is a reflection of past learning and is understandable given the various reasonable parental belief-systems; or (3) the symptom serves a broader function or purpose within the family and is possibly a metaphoric reflection of deeper underlying hidden agendas, dysfunctions, or dynamics.

Initially, I assume that behavior is just behavior, and I try not to make unwarranted assumptions about any behavior. I start off by dealing with the problem simply and pragmatically. At the same time, don't be naive; you need to keep other options and possibilities in the back of your mind. Learn as much as you can about the symptoms from a systemic point of view, and be sensitive and intuitive to what the symptoms might represent. Ask yourself, "Is there some broader context, understanding, dynamics, or meaning to these symptoms?" Be sure to start with the simple and move to the more complex, but consider the possibilities before setting up an intervention. For example, if a step-daughter runs away from home or is truant from school, as simple as it might be, it's possible that she was interested in being truant on just that day and believed that she could get away with it; or maybe she just wanted to "try her wings" and be independent. In any case, don't try to set up an intervention to stop the daughter from running away from home without first exploring and becoming aware of the broader issues and context of the family. It may be that the step-father is trying to "put the moves" on the step-daughter and that she is trying to escape the situation. Don't be naive; be aware of the possible context and take precautions. But don't look for major dysfunction and pathology in every symptom, either.

With all the current problems of sexual abuse, physical abuse, and alcohol and drug abuse, you can't afford to be naive, and these factors must be considered before embarking on a particular intervention plan. Although you must be aware of the possible broader, contextual, symbolic, and metaphoric parameters of inappropriate behavior, don't get locked into looking for, thinking that there must be, those broader issues in every case. As Freud observed, "Sometimes, a cigar is just a cigar."

With most simple and situationally inappropriate behavior, whether in the school, the home, or both, the cigar is just a cigar and the behavior can be stopped easily with clear directions and appropriate follow-through or back-ups. If this approach doesn't work, then you can move to the next level and conceptualize the behavior from a more complex perspective.

From this second perspective, you can conceptualize the student or child as one who has learned that he can act inappropriately and get away with it because there is some type of direct or indirect support for the behavior from within the system. Under these circumstances, there are usually parental, personal, and/or philosophical beliefs that are helping to maintain the inappropriate behavior. These beliefs need to be systematically explored, and if the counselor is successful at helping the parents or teachers to erode those beliefs and see that there is little or no evidence to support their contentions, then you will also see fairly quick changes. Remember, most parents do things for reasonable reasons. We

Other Helpful Concepts, Ideas, and Belief-Systems   101

are not looking for villains or someone to fix the blame on. Our job is to help the parents see where their beliefs are coming from, see that they have been acting congruently with those beliefs, and see that even though they have been reasonable beliefs, they have had the unfortunate consequence of allowing the child to have an excuse to continue to act inappropriately.

Most cases which we have to deal with in schools fit within one of these two options. However, again, you will get cases in which the third option—the symptomatic behavior being a reflection of deeper family issues—is more predominantly in play. In these cases you will need to be sensitive, use some of your clinical intuitions, and explore the possibilities before you institute your interventions for change.

Depending on your training and experience in working with families at this third level, the time factor involved, and the level of dysfunction in the family, you might need to refer the family for outside private family counseling. However, do not assume that just because the family problems appear to be complex that you can't help to solve them. Even if you have to refer the family for outside counseling, the parents still have to take a stand on their child's school-related problems. So try the model and see if you can help the family in this area.

Transgenerational Issues

Transgenerational issues broaden your perspective and understanding of the presenting problem as it might relate to previous generations in the family. How are the parents', or possibly the grandparents' influences involved with the symptom-bearer, the problem or issue at hand? In this school-based family-counseling approach, you won't need to get into any major transgenerational psychotherapeutic process or analysis. It isn't always necessary to delve into the past in great detail on every case. Keep it simple. If a student is truant from school, ask the parents why they think the student is missing school. They may say, "Because he's bored." Question the parent.

Counselor: Were you ever bored in school? (transgenerational probe—parent's reaction)
Parent: Oh, sure; I was bored in school all the time.
Counselor: Did you get to leave school?

Parent: I couldn't leave school; it wasn't allowed back in those days.

Counselor: So 'boring' might not have much to do with it? How did your parents handle you with regard to this issue? (transgenerational probe—grandparents' reaction)

Parent: My parents just wouldn't let me ditch school.

Counselor: How did you feel about that?

Parent: I didn't like it at the time, but it was for the best.

Counselor: Let me see if I understand this. Your parents wouldn't allow you to leave school even though you didn't like it and you were bored. Now your son doesn't like school and he is bored, but it's okay for him to leave school?

This simple process begins to clarify the structure of the three generations. When using this family-counseling model, just quickly look at how the previous two generations dealt with the particular school-related problem of the identified patient (*e.g.*, missing school, getting F's, talking back to the teacher). This is done to see if you can get some ideas, insights, or hunches into why the parents currently hold the belief-systems they hold and why they communicate and interact in the ways that they do.

Many times when parents are asked transgenerational questions, such as how their parents dealt with certain issues or how they responded to their parents attempts to control them over that issue, they will tell you that their parents were very stern, very authoritarian, that they hated the way their parents influenced them, that they didn't like their father, that they've never forgiven their parents for treating them in such and such a way, and that they swore if they ever had children they would never raise their kids the way their parents raised them. This information will further help to develop your hunches and hypotheses. Use this information to reframe their answers and to clarify what has been happening within the family.

As an example, you might say, "It sounds like you really care about your child, love him, and want him to get a good education. It appears to me that based on how you feel about how your parents raised you, you made a decision that you weren't going to act the same way that your Dad acted toward you. Based on that decision it seems that you've bent over backwards not to be authoritarian, but now your child is missing school, having problems, and is not being successful. Is that okay with you?"

"No, it's not okay; I love him and want him to do well."

"Is there a way you can help your child get back on task and help him to be successful in school without having to be unreasonable or authoritarian; to show him that you love him but that you also have to set some limits?"

Keep the transgenerational issues focused on the very limited nature of the student's presenting problems within the school context. Bring out the *reasonableness* of the parent's beliefs, hopes, and interaction patterns, especially in relation to their own family of origin. Again, don't go into great depth with the transgenerational family issues. Keep the topic focused but get enough information to understand the reasonableness of the parent's behavior, and then get back to the goal for the identified patient—the student being successful in school.

Ask yourself, "How does this transgenerational information relate to the presenting problem, and how can I use it to: understand the reasonableness of the parents actions; reframe or relabel the interaction patterns; and/or develop better intervention strategies based on it?" Always return to the present, and refocus on the student's success, and use this new information to have the parents come up with alternative ways to interact with their son that would better maximize the chances of achieving their goal.

The concept of transgenerational issues is a very important one because it allows you to get at some of the more significant beliefs and belief-systems that parents have but usually don't bring up immediately. Many of the parents' belief-systems are tied to those of their own parents, and their own families of origin. What they think, feel, and believe in terms of right or wrong, and what they should or shouldn't do in terms of raising their own children, many times stem from their own family of origin.

Again, my general suggestion is, within the school/family counseling context, keep things focused and simple; if that doesn't work, then get more complex in your thinking. Some system theorists look at transgenerational issues in a more involved and complex way. For example, they may see the mother's "assumed incompetence" in relation to the child as a scripting by some complex projection process and psychodynamic of the mother's family of origin; it may be some interlocking triangulation of at least three generations; it may be that the mother is "incompetent" to make the father feel important as the head of the family or to get the mother's mother involved in the parenting; it may be a question of boundary-setting—grandparents intruding and being overly involved in the parenting because the husband isn't supporting his wife and helping to make the family boundaries clear, which then contributes to making the wife seem incompetent. There are hundreds of ways to see and conceptualize transgenerational issues or behavior; the important thing is, can you use that information in a therapeutic way to help to create some family change in a more positive direction? If you would like some more information on transgenerational issues or family generational boundaries, I recommend that you read material on family histories and genograms, some of Bowen's or Minuchin's work, and some of the more psychodynamic family-systems therapists (references in Appendix A).

Reframing, or Relabeling

Reframing, or relabeling, is a concept that many therapeutic approaches use. It is forming a different conceptualization, a different way of seeing things, putting a different label on behavior—either on the parent's behavior or on the student's behavior. The counselor tries to benignly relabel the behavior, traits, characteristics, or interaction patterns of the family members so that they are not seen in hostile, authoritarian, or negative terms. The counselor tries to create a positive perspective, or a slightly different perspective, so that people will see the behavior in a different light. This relabeling process, if accepted, will benefit not only the person who is sending the old message or label, but also the person or persons receiving the message. In this manner, the relabeled behavior can be used or played in either direction to help to modify typical interaction patterns which, hopefully, will then help to change the family.

If the father comes on in a fairly controlling manner to the child or adolescent, you can label that as a way of saying that the parent is very concerned, has a strong sense of value, really cares about him or loves him. However, since the father has not influenced his son in the positive way that he would like, he is naturally hurt and is starting to come on stronger in an attempt to influence his son in a more positive direction. If the parent buys into this new label and accepts it, and the student is hearing this at the same time, then the student, as well as the father, is also getting a slightly different perspective.

Then say to the student, "When you hear Dad coming on strong, are you seeing this as hurt, caring, love, and concern, or are you seeing it as he's just getting on your back?" The student usually sees it as getting on his back. So you reply, "Ahh, so there's a mismatch in the way you two are looking at this. Can you now see that Dad is. . . ?"

If appropriate, ask the family about how they express concern, love, tenderness, and caring, and how they express hurt and anger over disappointment. Ask the parents how their parents handled some of these issues (transgenerational probe). This will give you a lot of new information, and, depending on which way it goes, you can use this new information to develop ideas about what is going on in the family and relabel some of the interactions accordingly. Get Mom involved in this discussion and relabeling process, too. Many times the mother will say Dad's too hard on the boy, and then she feels that she has to be lenient to compensate for the father's hard-nosed position. This compensation leads to a never-ending cycle of the parents pushing each other into extreme positions (too strict/too lenient) that neither likes. This cycle needs to be broken.

To help stop this destructive cycle, turn to the mother and ask, "Mom, when Dad does this . . . and your son does this . . ., how do you interpret it?" "Do you see Dad's style of communicating to his son as concern, or as coming on strong?" "Did you know how all of this related to your husband's family of origin and how painful this was for your husband?" "Can you now see he really does care about his son so much so that it hurts him to see his son not being successful?" "What do you want your son to do?" "How can you and your husband work together to help your son achieve this goal?" By relabeling, she'll hopefully see the father/son interaction in a slightly different light and will then be more willing to work with the father to help to achieve the desired goal. It is essential that this process also be done from the mother's perspective so that the father will perceive her differently, and thus be more willing to work together with her. The goal is to get the two parents working together and setting some reasonable limits for their child's behavior.

If you can, tie the relabels back to the transgenerational issues: "How did your Dad deal with this?" "How did your Mom deal with this?" "How did you feel about it?" Then you can say to the father, "So, your Dad came on pretty hard, too, and you didn't like it. Now the pattern is repeating itself: You are coming on pretty hard, and your son doesn't like it. What would you like to have happen differently for your son?" "Can you now see that this might have been the way your father showed that he cared?" "What would you have liked your Dad to have said and done for you?" You try to bring all these aspects and ideas together into a theme to help to create a new family reality, a new way of looking at things.

I conceptualize reframing, or relabeling, as the counselor's attempt to persuade the family to see their typical interactions, labels, name-calling, traits, or attributes from a slightly different perspective. The counselor attempts to give them a more positive and benign interpretation, with the hope that they will then act differently toward each other. Labeling a specific behavior, phenomenon, or person becomes a way of both seeing things and not seeing things. Once someone has locked into labeling a trait or characteristic in a certain way, he then tends to see that behavior in the person, and it becomes a self-fulfilling prophecy. Once someone says, "The child is lazy," it helps to set their perception of that person. Once the label is set, the labeler has a tendency to overlook or ignore all the other ways the child is acting or behaving. They seem to zero in on the times when the child is lazy, which then proves their point and keeps the self-fulfilling prophecy going. When you question and erode parental belief-systems, you set up some uncertainty and confusion on the parents' part. This process of confusion and uncertainty then makes it easier for the counselor to suggest alternative explanations or relabels. If the parents are not sure why the child is acting the way he is, there is some confusion, ambiguity and uncertainty as to what is happening, and why. This then leaves you some maneuvering room to help the family to change and to come up with new labels.

Under these confusing conditions, people have a tendency to search out new information in order to form closure, to form a new sense of security and reality for themselves. The counselor, by giving the parents some new labels, traits, or new ways of seeing things, has given the parents the opportunity to see things differently and to develop in a more positive direction. By creating some cognitive dissonance, you're getting the parents to a point of uncertainty. They can no longer use the same old beliefs and labels. They are no longer sure. At this time, if you happen to suggest alternatives, reframe the behavior, reframe the context, or relabel the behavior in a more benign positive direction, you will have created more leverage and flexibility to further change the family and the family-interaction patterns.

The relabeling technique can be used not only to relabel typical interactions so that participants might see things from a different perspective, but it can also be used to inhibit, or block, typical family-interaction patterns. The presentation and acceptance of the new label helps to prevent the family from falling back into their typical interactions, labeling and name-calling. For example, if you encounter a father/son relationship that typically escalates into negative, harmful behavior patterns, and if you have successfully relabeled the father as a caring, loving dad who does not know how to show his love as well as he would like to (partly because of his family of origin), and if you have relabeled the adolescent's "rebellion" as his inappropriate way of protecting his parents, especially his dad, from having to experience the pain of having to separate or leave the family on a positive note, then you have helped to create a context which inhibits future negative interactions.

Once the label is in place, it is like the statement, "Don't think of the word 'elephant' for the next thirty seconds." Every time the father and son now interact in their typical ways, the relabels will come to mind, cause them to pause, and then, it is hoped, remind them to interact in a more positive direction. To help to insure that the family interact in a more positive way and to avoid getting trapped in the old labels, name-calling, and beliefs, you can encourage the family to talk right now in the counseling session about some of these relabeled issues (*e.g.*, gaining independence, showing love, protecting each other from pain, dealing with hurt and anger, coping with uncertainty and disappointment). If you are an advocate of paradoxical techniques, at this point you might suggest to the father and son that within the next few weeks they are going to have a serious argument in an attempt to get them to *really* understand and know each other. But since they have had a history of misinterpreting each other's messages, you want them, as a homework assignment, to prepare for this upcoming argument by having daily small-scale arguments for the next week so that they can *really* get in touch and learn what the *real* issues are so that when the big argument occurs they can express themselves in a healthier way. When giving directions to the family, give them in very specific, concrete terms. (For more information on how to do this, please see references to the works of Haley and Madanes under the sub-heading "Strategic Family Therapy" in Appendix A: Bibliography.)

Again, even though you might explore some of several issues, keep the focus on the problem and the solution. If the parents can get the student to go to school, stay in school, and get at least straight C's, most families do not have to fight over the student's failing grades.

For additional information on reframing, refer to Jim Alexander's *Functional Family Therapy,* Salvador Minuchin's *Structural Family Therapy, Family Therapy,* and *Family Therapy Techniques,* and Virginia Satir's *Conjoint Family Therapy* and *People Making* (also noted in Appendix A).

Chapter V: Case Study

After you have experience with the model and completely understand the structure and logic of it, you can develop your own style, without always following the stages of therapy in exact order. As you gain experience with the methods and techniques, you will become more flexible about using your personal style to achieve the desired result. You will also adapt more comfortably from the formal stages of the model to "process information" that presents itself in the session. You will also learn how to use that information to illustrate your points without necessarily having to continue through the remaining formal steps of the model.

This demonstration case study is a re-creation of an actual case. Because the model is structured and sequential, this particular case works well for training purposes and allows for my comments on typical questioning techniques that arise in counseling.

In this case an adolescent boy was failing high school and was referred to me by the school counselor. As the school psychologist, I worked with the family in an initial family-counseling session and then held a follow-up telephone session two weeks later. At the initial session I met the student and both his parents. We socialized for a few minutes and then began the session.

Step One: Identifying The Goal of Therapy

What is the problem and how will you determine when it is solved?

> *(C = counselor's comments; M = mother's comments; F = father's comments; S = son's comments; P = parents' comments.)*

C: John, what difficulties are your parents having in getting you to do what they want you to do?
S: I don't have any problems; it's just my parents. They're always on my back.
C: I understand that you feel like your parents are on your back, and I know you feel like you don't have any problems, especially the way you see it right now. However, I asked you what problems do your parents have in getting you to do what they want?
S: Going to school and getting good grades.
C: (to parents) Is this the way you see the problem, also?
P: Yes, pretty much so.
F: He's not going to school, and he's failing....
M: He's always "ditching class" (this is a California term meaning truant, absent), and we keep telling him that if he doesn't go to school and get a good education, he'll never amount to anything. He's always causing trouble....

(Both parents start one of their favorite lectures and scripts: the kid is no good; here are all the awful things he has done; we keep telling him, but what can you do with such an awful kid? The mother appears to be more intense and emotionally involved than the father. At this point, you need to stop the parents from giving scripts or long lectures about the student's actions. Instead, have the parents focus on the problem and its solution. This maneuver is somewhat risky because you don't want to lose the parents and be seen as siding with the student against the parents. Be careful, especially this early in the session.)

C: (Holding up hand to the parents) Excuse me for interrupting. I don't want to be impolite or disrespectful, but I want to check on something very important. (Counselor turns to son.) Do you know what your mom and dad are going to say?
S: Yes. I've heard it a million times before.
C: Could you please tell me in a few words what message your Mom and Dad want to get across to you?

S: Yeah. Go to school and get good grades, so you don't become a bum.
C: (to parents) Is this basically what you were going to say?
P: Yes.
C: Okay. John is a pretty smart youngster, and he knows what you want him to do, but he's just not doing it. So, what is it then that your son has to start doing that he is not doing now, or what is it that he has to stop doing that he is doing now? (Don't waste time listening to the parents tell how awful their son's behavior is; refocus parental attention on to the problem and a solution. You have to protect the student from being "dumped on", but at the same time you don't want to alienate the parents. It is strategic to side with the parents, while keeping them focused on a healthy solution to the problem.)
M: He knows what we want, and he should know better. He is 16 years old and needs to take responsibility for his own actions.

(The "should" problem needs to be clarified, as well as the abstract term "responsibility".)

C: Yes, I agree with you. He should know better, but he has given you a very clear message by his actions that he is not going to do it on his own. I assume by his words and actions that it is no problem to him. Is it a problem for both of you? If so, what do you want changed? (Structure of technique: "I agree . . .," [parental support or joining] "but . . ." [kick to reality, then refocus to the possible solution to the problem].)
M: I want him to grow up and be more responsible and mature.

("Responsible" and "mature" need to be defined in concrete and specific terms, so everyone knows what is meant by them.)

C: I'm not sure exactly what you mean. "Grow up" and "be more responsible and mature" are rather abstract terms and can mean different things to different people. I want to make sure I understand you correctly. What is it in concrete terms that John has to do so that when he does it, he will know, you will know, and your husband will know that he is grown up, responsible, and mature? (kick—support—refocus)

M: Well, I want him to try to bring his grades up.

("I want" might mean a simple preference, or it might indicate a demand—no choice. "Try" means he really does not have to do it. It also reflects a parental belief of incapability that needs to be drawn out later in the session. Don't get into any analysis of beliefs yet, even if the parents spontaneously give you some. You need to get the goal down in concrete terms first.)

C: When you say "try" to bring his grades up, do you mean that he has to bring his grades up or just give it a few tries? If it doesn't work out, is it okay to quit? (When asking questions, whenever possible, give a few options and have the parents clarify the situation. In this way you don't force them to defend themselves. "I really want to understand. Is it more like this . . ., or is it more like this . . . ?")

M: No, he *has* to bring his grades up.

C: So, it is not a question of trying. He has to bring up his grades. No choice?

M: Yes, no choice.

C: When you said "I want" this to happen, were you conveying a message of "My preference is that you get better grades," "I hope and prefer that you get better grades, but that is your choice", or "Get better grades, no choice"?

M: He must get better grades—no choice!

C: And when his grades are up, will you consider him more grown up and mature? (Follow up on previous issues and try to bring them to closure.)

M: Well, it's not just the grades, but it's his attitude, too. He has a lousy attitude.

(Again, another abstract term that needs to be behaviorally defined.)

C: What is he doing that makes you think he has a lousy attitude?

M: He always talks back to me. I ask him to do something at home, and he never does a thing without a big fight. He is lazy.

Case Study 113

(She starts off behaviorally, but then she falls back to trait attribution and labels him "lazy". The label "lazy" needs to be questioned or changed to a more benign label.)

C: (to the mother) I suspect that John really does a lot of activities such as swimming, playing basketball or soccer, hanging out and talking to his friends.

C: (asks the son) Do you do a lot of things with your friends—run around, play sports, things like that?

S: Yeah. I play soccer and swim, and I have a lot of friends.

C: (tells Mom) He is not really lazy. He is probably just very inactive at times. The real issue appears to be that he just isn't doing *what* you want him to do *when* you want him to do it. What does he have to do differently—in concrete terms—so when he does it, you will think he has a good attitude and is not so inactive? (This was, perhaps, an awkward attempt to reframe and relabel the mother's perception of her son's "laziness". Even though this was not a smooth interaction and relabel, it attenuates the mother's perception and the son's as well.)

M: I want him to go to school, improve his grades, take out the trash, and clean up his room when I ask him to—all without talking back to me.

(You may get a long list of problems. Have the parents decide which is the most important to them and the one they wish to work on first.)

C: Let's work on one of these areas and solve that problem. Then you can apply some of the same techniques to these other areas if you wish to solve them. Out of all of these things you mentioned, which one is the most important to both of you, and which one would you like to work on first?

M: Improving his school work and grades.

(You need to find out what "improvement" means. To what standard? However, before you do that, you need to check with Dad to see what he thinks about the problem.)

C: (to the father) Do you agree that this is the major problem and the one that you want to work on first?

F: Yes.

(Dad, at this point, does not really sound convincing. My feeling at this time was that Dad was in a state of ambivalent agreement. Going into the counseling session, I knew that the father was an engineer and vice-president of one of the local aerospace companies. My initial impression of the man, right or wrong, was that he was a "strong, silent type", pragmatic, somewhat rigid, a facts-and-figures man, not big on feelings, and, definitely, not big on psychology or any type of personal analysis. Based partly on my impressions of the man and the fact that I didn't have any concrete information about where he was coming from, I didn't challenge him. I accepted his statement at face value and went on as if it were a strong affirmation. Part of the reason for this was that all through the mother's statements, Dad had been in little tiny motions, nodding his head in agreement.)

C: (to both parents) Okay, when you say "improving his school work", what do you mean?
M: Go to school and get at least straight C's.

(You need to get very specific, pinpointing the what, when, where, and how of everything.)

C: Let's explore this a little. John, do you go to school now?
S: Yeah, for the most part.
C: So you go to school and then leave? The old "in one door and out the other door" trick?
S: Yeah.
M: I see what you are getting at. I want him to go to school, stay in school without ditching, and I want him to do his work in school.
C: Great! You're really getting the idea. Go to school, and stay in school. Now, what about this ditching? I know a lot of families who say that it's okay to ditch school every once in awhile, just as long as they know about it. In fact I know some parents who will write the absence notes for the students if the circumstances are right. This is no real problem to me, just as long as the family agrees. Can there be any ditching, and if so, under what circumstances? What are the parameters?

(This tactic encourages the family to tell you the truth, and to help set the real limits of the student's behavior.)

P: No, no way, not under any circumstances. (Both Dad and Mom were very clear on this point.)

C: Okay. Now what about the C's? If he gets C's, are you going to, in his words, "get off his back"?

(Determine what the real message is. Is there a hidden agenda? Will the parents really be satisfied?)

S: No, she will want me to get B's and then A's.

(This is another good reason to have everyone in the counseling session. They help each other to validate reality. The son intuitively knows what the message really is.)

C: I see. (Counselor turns toward mother.) Is that so?
M: Well, yes!
C: So, what is the real message here? What does he have to do, no choice, so that you will feel that he is back on track?
M: I just want him to do his best so he can get ahead in the world.

(One's best is an abstraction and needs to be clarified. Also, you can relabel mother's being "on her son's back" behavior as "love", "care", "protection", "concern", and so on, if you wish.)

C: I see. I get the feeling, Mom, that you love your son very much, and you want to protect him from future hardship by having him do well in school now. The problem is we can all improve in almost everything we do, but most of us never do our best in everything all the time. So, what are your standards, what is your bottom line for John—the standard which you and your husband can live with—the one that John has no choice but to do, and the one that you two are willing to make happen?
M: I prefer A's and B's, but the bottom line is nothing below straight C's.

(Up to this point, Mom has done most of the talking. Be aware that this might reflect other issues that are going on in the family. There are a number of possibilities or hypotheses that need to be tested by gathering more information: (1) Mom could be overly involved with the boy; (2) Dad could be supporting the boy against the mother and sabotaging her efforts; (3) Mom might be setting the boy up so Dad would have to get more involved with her; (4) both Mom and Dad have some hidden belief-systems of their own that might make their behavior reasonable; (5) the boy really has interpersonal intra-psychic problems and is out to get his parents; or (6) the boy's problems are a reflection of deeper family or marital problems.

Consider the possibilities as you gather more information. As the information accumulates, you will refine your hypotheses. Up to this point I think that Mom and Dad basically have a good marriage, have no major psychopathology, but are not sure what the best way is to get their son to do his homework. So until proven otherwise, I operate on this assumption.)

C: Do you agree with that, Dad?
F: Yes, I think C's are fine. (Mom gives Dad a knowing grin.)
C: (to mother) I noticed a special look to Dad. What did that mean?
M: Jim is gone a lot and, I feel, doesn't support me much on this grade issue.

(Mom believes that Dad is gone a lot, which can be explored later in the "analysis of beliefs" (Step Two) after you have firmly set the goal. Fact: Dad does not support her as much as she wants on the grade issue. Start thinking about how you can work with this information to achieve the goal if it becomes a major issue later in the counseling session.)

F: I just don't think it is quite as important as she makes it. It's not the end of the world if he doesn't get straight A's.

(When it becomes clear that the student has been getting two different messages from his parents, you need to question and clarify this. Since this family was sharp, I decided to question these differences from a cognitive perspective rather than on a more experiential base (see pp. 135-139). The real trick, however, is to find out why the parents have been acting the way they have, relabel any derogatory labels to a more benign position, and create some interventions that might change the situation.

No matter why the parents disagree, persuade them to come to some agreement. Don't look for villains, or blame either parent. Remember, people's behavior is reasonable given their beliefs. Have hope, and work for change. Also, remember that even if there are strong differences between parents, for the most part they love their children and want the best for them. Focus on their common concern and love for their children, and emphasize that education is an important way to show that love.)

C: What do the two of you agree upon that is absolutely important in terms of John's education, that you are willing to support each other on, and that is neccessary to make sure he is successful in school? This will show John that both of you love and care about him so much that you will not let him fail in school.

P: Straight C's.

(You get tentative agreement on a joint goal. At this point, you are not sure if the parents are just going along with you or whether they are really committed. You must probe to find out if this is a reasonable request and get a firmer commitment from them. If you get evidence and support for the goal from both parents, you'll strengthen their commitment to pursue the goal, no matter what other issues may be going on in the home.)

C: Is John capable of getting straight C's?
P: Yes. Oh, yes.
M: He is capable of much more than that. That's why I get so upset with him.

(Check the evidence they have to support this belief. Again, as they give you more information, the commitment to the goal should increase.)

C: You have evidence to support this?
M: Yes. In elementary school and junior-high school he got A's and B's.
F: His school achievement test scores are all above average; he was tested for some gifted program, and his IQ is way above average.
C: Okay. You have evidence that he is very capable, and the goal is to get John to go to school, stay in school, and get straight C's—nothing less. Is that straight C's in all subjects? P.E.? Art?
P: Yes.
C: Can that be an A in one subject and an F in another, to average out to a C?
P: No way! It must be straight C's.

C: Straight C's for how long? A semester, a year, or the rest of his school career?
P: The rest of his school career.
C: Based on the evidence you have just presented, it is reasonable to request that he get C's, and, if I understand you right, both of you expect this goal to be achieved throughout the rest of his schooling.
P: Yes.
C: See if I understand this correctly. You would prefer that he achieve better grades than C's, but you are not willing to make him get straight A's or B's because that would have to be his choice. However, you are willing to support each other, and, if necessary, go to any lengths to ensure that he gets straight C's. Is that pretty much the picture?
P: Yes.
C: So, if John gets at least straight C's in all subjects for the rest of his high-school career and doesn't ditch another day of school, then you will know this goal has been successful and has been attained, is that it?
P: Yes.

(You now have completed Step One and are ready for Step Two, analysis of parental belief systems.)

Step Two: Analysis of Beliefs
C: Okay. What do you think accounts for the fact that John has not been getting straight C's and has been ditching school? What ideas or thoughts have crossed your mind?

(You need to assure some parents that they don't have to come up with the absolute truth or cause. Passing thoughts or feelings are sometimes helpful. The intent is to make the implicit explicit. The student needs to hear these various ideas even though later on he discovers that they don't necessarily hold true.)

M: Well... I don't know....
C: Is John dumb?

(One of my ice-breakers. I already know the answer from the previous information the parents have given me, but this will get them going.)

P: No. No.

F: No way.
M: He's a smart boy.
C: He knows how to read and write. He doesn't have any learning disabilities?

(In this particular case, there are no problems, but in other cases you must be prepared to question what evidence they have to support his disabilities and draw out counter-information that supports his abilities to learn.)

M: No, nothing like that. He reads above grade level. He's a smart kid.
C: Is he crazy or emotionally ill?

(I usually ask this question directly because of the implied assumption that anyone who goes to see a psychologist is mentally ill. I wish to make the implicit explicit and have the parents dispel the notion or try to support it.)

P: (both parents very emphatically) No way: he isn't crazy!
C: Well, great. I ask that because sometimes when parents take their children to see a psychologist, the child thinks that the parents must see him as crazy or something.
S: Yeah! I told them before we came here that I didn't want to come to see you. They could save their time and money because I wasn't crazy.

(The student knew or felt the implicit message.)

C: Well, at least it's good to know that you're not crazy, sick, or emotionally ill.
S: Boy, you said it.

(Sometimes I drive this point home even more if I sense that the youngster is really going through some major changes and is questioning his own mental or emotional state. Depending on the situation, I might directly ask the parents when they were growing up, or even now as adults, if the thought ever crossed their minds that they might be a little bit crazy, not normal, or not able to fit in with the crowd. Usually, the answer is an overwhelming "YES". I then ask them if they have ever talked this over or shared this doubt with their son. We might talk about the subject in the session for a while. I might share my "expert" thoughts on the matter. All of this discussion is carried out to "normalize" the process, situation, or thoughts.)

M: He is definitely not crazy or anything like that. If anything, he is just lazy.

(Mom falls back on her old trait-attribute stance.)

C: You mentioned lazy before; do you mean . . . ?

M: (interrupting) Well, I don't mean "lazy" lazy. It's just that he doesn't do his work. In fact, if anything, he is kind of hyper.

(You would think these to be incompatible beliefs—lazy and hyperactive. However, the mother defines the term lazy to mean that he does not do what she wants him to do when she wants him to do it. Within this context, he can be very active and lazy simultaneously.)

C: What do you mean by "hyper"?

(Define everything, put it into behavioral terms, find out where she got the ideas.)

M: Well, he's always been a very active person, into everything. He never sits still, and his mind is always off on different tangents.

(At this point, you have a workable, behavioral definition of hyperactivity, and you want to start questioning beliefs. By the way, the boy had been sitting quietly with no signs of hyperactivity in the session—process information.)

C: How do you account for this hyperactivity? Is it genetic, biochemical, a result of excess sugar, what?

M: I don't know. I don't think it is genetic. It might be the sugar. I've read some articles on that, but I really think that's just the way boys are.

(Here are possible belief-systems: it's the sugar; it's just the way boys are.)

C: You believe that it might be the sugar—but it is more probable that it's "boys will be boys"?

M: Yes.

(Questions to erode the belief.)

C: Are all boys this way?

M: No.

C: Do you know some boys who are more active than John who get good grades and don't ditch?

M: Yes. I guess so.

Case Study

C: Do you know some boys less active than John who get good grades and don't ditch?
M: Yes.
C: Do you know some boys who are less active than John who get worse grades and ditch?
M: Yes.
C: How do you account for this?
M: (bewildered) I don't know.

(Her belief is now hopefully in doubt.)

C: You say John never sits still and is hyperactive, so I assume that he can't control himself. How do you account for the fact that he has been sitting here quietly for at least fifteen minutes to half an hour? If he is hyper and can't sit still, how do you explain the fact that he is sitting still? Does he have two types of biochemical systems, one to turn the sugar on and one to turn the sugar off?

(You need to notice what's going on in the session and move to process information when appropriate.)

M: Well, he was hyper when he was younger, in elementary school. He is still very active, but he is able to control himself now that he is older.

(Another popular belief is that children grow out of hyperactivity, usually after puberty. However, this belief is inconsistent with information previously given by the parents.)

C: I see. You said that in elementary school he got good grades. How is it that he was hyper in elementary school and *unable* to control himself, yet got good grades, and now that he is *able* to control himself, he is ditching and getting poor grades?
M: I don't know. I just don't know. I know that John is a very smart boy, and maybe he is just bored with school. You know, a lot of teachers are there just for their paychecks.

(This new excuse for letting the boy get out of doing his work was probably one that the boy himself provided. Even if true, is it okay for him to continue to act the way he has been acting?)

C: For the sake of argument, let's say that is true. The teachers are there just for their paychecks, and your son

really is bored. Is it okay, then, for him never to do any homework, to flunk out of school and get poor grades?
P: No.

(It's time to explore possible transgenerational issues while continuing to erode the excuse of boredom. This excuse, however, provides a logical transition to get more information from Dad.)

C: (to mother) Were you ever bored with school?
M: I liked school a lot, but, yes, I was bored at times.
C: Did you ditch and get F"s?
M: No way. My parents would have killed me.

(Structure: She was bored, but parents didn't let her ditch and get poor grades; he is bored, but parents let him fail.)

C: (to father) Were you ever bored in school?
F: Yes, but you see, I had different circumstances. I didn't do well in high school. I dropped out and went into the Navy, but that was because I had to. My dad was an alcoholic, and we were poor. We had a lot of fights in our family, and I had to get out of the house.

(It becomes clear that the father's family background might have something to do with the dynamics of the boy's school performance. For right now, however, you want to stay with the issue of boredom and school performance.)

C: (to father) After you got out of the Navy, what did you do?

(I knew that the family was affluent and that the father was in a high-management position with a large aerospace company. I wanted to find out how he got from being a high-school dropout to that position and, at the same time, stay with the issue of boredom.)

F: I went back to school and got a college degree in engineering, with straight A's.
C: Boy! That's really impressive. I'm sure it took a lot of hard work and sacrifice on your part to be as successful as you are today. Were you ever bored with some of your college classes, even though you got straight A's?
F: Yes, sometimes. But I had to take the courses to get the degree—and, besides, by then I knew what I wanted, and I wanted to do well.

(Possible beliefs to keep in mind about why the Dad is behaving as he is: believes that son is going through a stage of development; believes that only self-motivated students do well; believes that students should make their own decisions; believes that it's possible to drop out of school and still succeed; believes that he will be like his parents if he makes demands. While considering these possible reasons for the father's behavior toward the boy, you still have to focus on eroding the belief that boredom causes ditching and poor grades.)

C: Okay, so being bored does not necessarily mean you have to get poor grades. Both of you have been bored in school before, and you both did okay. I suspect that even now both of you get bored at times and don't like doing certain things, but you do them.
P: Yeah. I can see that.
C: Perhaps even at work.
F: Yes, that's true.

(At this point, I can guess at what's going on. I'm probably not telling the family anything they don't already know or haven't thought about at some level. I continue in this manner not to interpret the behavior but to explore the family belief systems and to further erode them.)

C: You know, as I listen to all of this, I have a hunch. Correct me if I am wrong. I feel that John really identifies with his dad in some ways, and he knows that Dad didn't do so well in high school, but he turned out great. He has a college degree, a great job, and is doing very well. John also knows he is pretty smart, and that he'll be able to turn it around just like his dad did.
M: In a way, that is true. The two of them are alike in a lot of ways.

(Belief: like father, like son. Possible genetic or social learning theory basis. Another possible hypothesis to keep in the back of your mind is this: Mom doesn't like certain characteristics in Dad, sees them in the boy, and takes it out on him instead of directly relating to the father. This, at the time, was a low-level possibility in my mind. If, however, the future intervention did not work, you could always come back to this hypothesis, as well as others, and explore them with the family and develop new and more complex interventions.)

F: (emphatically) Yes. But it is different these days. Technology is different. You have to get a good education. Times have changed. Besides that, I'm not a drunk, kicking him out of the house, like my father was. I'm not setting unreasonable standards and then belittling him for not achieving them. I care about and love my children.

(This is a very important disclosure on the father's part. It sheds some light on the transgenerational issues and the boy's current school performance. It shows some possible reasons why the father has acted the way he has, not pushing his son too much as his father did. It lends logical and emotional support to the position that he is willing to take some positive action to ensure his son's success. It also gives you a great lead-in for a relabeling of future parental structure and involvement to make sure that the student is successful— care and love.)

C: So, both of you really care about and love John, and you don't want to risk having him fail in high school, even though you know he might make it on his own if he wants to at a later date.

F: Yes, but the chances of being successful are lower these days, and there is no use taking the risk.

(The father gives more evidence of commitment to do something. At this point, I challenge the parents in an effort to get them to agree, take charge, and do something to stop John's inappropriate behavior.)

C: Well, John is giving both of you a very clear message that he is willing to take the chance, as evidenced by the fact that he has not been doing his work on his own. Are you both willing to let him make that decision and fail?

P: (emphatically) No. No way.

C: So, that is not negotiable?

F: That's right. He no longer has any choice to fail.

M: Yes, he must pass high-school. If he doesn't want to go on to college, that is his choice. We're not trying to run his life, but he can't fail high-school.

C: Okay, both of you are in agreement. He can't fail high-school, he has no choice in that matter, and we are back to the goal of getting at least straight C's.

P: Yes.
C: You're not interested in setting unreasonable demands or running your son's life. You want him to be independent and successful; but, in this one area of his life, because you love him, you will not let him fail. Is that correct?
P: Yes.
C: (to the father) You're not setting unreasonably high standards, getting drunk, or kicking your son out of the house. You care about John, you love him, and you will help him to be successful. Is that correct?
F: Yes.

(I'm hoping to make the father see a difference between setting unreasonable standards, and acting in unreasonable, hurtful, authoritarian ways, versus, setting reasonable standards, and acting in reasonable, caring, loving, authoritative ways. Retrospectively, this would have been a good time to make this point even clearer by asking the father directly if he saw the difference. It would also have been a good place to ask him if he saw why he has been reasonably reluctant to set the standards and back them up, and if the wife now understood why the father had not supported her quite as much as she would have liked.)

C: Is there anything else that either of you thought of that might account for John's not doing his work?
M: No. . . . (long pause)

(I give the parents time to think. If nothing comes up, I go back to some of the previous information given and/or question the parents about any hunches I might have.)

C: You mentioned that Dad is gone a lot.
M: Yes, but I think I understand what you are getting at, and that does not really account for it. I know other dads who are gone a lot and the kids get good grades.
C: Great, it looks like you're seeing that there is really no excuse. I've worked with a lot of single mothers where Dad is gone a lot either because of death or divorce, and most of them are very successful at getting their children to do want they want them to do.
M: Yeah, I can see that now.
C: What about drugs or alcohol; do you think these might account for his behavior?

(This is a double-edged question designed for both the student and the parents, especially since the father had mentioned that his father was an alcoholic. Usually I ask this question in a vague way so that the family is not sure if I'm asking about the student or the parents. Then I watch carefully for any clues. Besides, listening to what they might say and what evidence they might have to support their position, I also watch for any non-verbal clues to explore so that by the time I'm finished I am fairly satisfied that substance abuse is not part of the problem.)

P/S: (together) *No way!*

(At this point, I'm ready to move on to Step Three, even though I consider the possibility that there might be a hidden agenda or belief system that has not been explored yet.)

Step Three: What Have You Tried Before to Solve the Problem?

C: Okay, what have you tried in the past to get him to be successful at school?

M: You name it, and we have tried it: talking to him, lecturing him, fighting with him, punishing him, restricting him, bribing him—$10 for every A—counseling. You name it, we've tried it. We went to another counselor once for a few sessions, and we talked about our feelings and who owned the problem (I could just imagine how excited the father was about that). We've tried it all.

(Although the parents tried many methods, each intervention included a choice for the student. You must get specific information. Have the parents provide concrete examples. Have them describe interactions, relating what they actually said; or, if you would like, have them enact what they said and did.)

C: You say you punish him, put him on restriction. What do you actually do and say? Give me an example.

M: I don't know. Something like: 'You have to get a good education. Your dad and I get really upset with you when you bring home poor grades like this. If you keep up this type of behavior, you're not going to get to do anything. You will be on restriction until your grades improve.' Usually, about that time, I get very angry and frustrated.

Case Study   127

(Analysis of communications: lecture—advantages of a good education; statement of fact—"your dad and I are upset"; "if/then" contracts—if no school work, then on restriction.)

C: Have any of these things worked?
M: No, not really.
C: Did you put him on restriction?

(I want to see if she follows through with her back-up, even though it is an if/then contract; if she can be trusted—if she means what she says, or if she lets him out of the consequences—and if she is successful at punishing him. If she was successful at punishing him, I can use that information in Step Four. If she was successful in punishing him, she can be successful in other areas.)

M: I've tried it, and I can keep him on it. But, after awhile it gets so he doesn't get to see anyone or do anything, and I think at times I'm creating a social isolate. So, I let him off the hook for good behavior.

(The mother is successful at keeping him on restriction, even though he does not like it, but is not successful in the school area. I keep this in mind and will come back to it later.)

C: In examining the situations you have mentioned, I noticed that you give John the choice as to whether he is going to behave. The choice is his: either he gets good grades, or you will punish him in some way.
F: Yes, that's about the way it is.
C: And it looks like John is saying to you very clearly that if given a choice, he'll take the punishment.
M: It sure seems that way.

(We're now ready for Step Four: Parental Successes.)

Step Four: Parental Successes

C: In what ways have you been successful in getting John to do what you want him to do when he has not wanted to do it?
S: Coming here!

(It's important to have everyone present in the session because you get information from everyone, and you never know from whom it will come.)

C: Did you want to come here?
S: No. This is stupid.

(I knew the answer before I asked the question, but I wanted the information to illustrate a point.)

C: (to parents) He did not want to be here, but you got him to come. How did you do that?
F: We just told him that he had no choice; he had to come.
C: I see. You were very successful when you told him he just had to do it. How else have you been successful?
M: I don't know.

(Many times parents have difficulty seeing their successes. Actively explore with the family the successes they have had, and make explicit the communications and techniques they have used when they were successful.)

C: Does John have chores around the house?
S: Boy, you said it! She has me doing. . . .
M: He never does them.
S: Yes, I do. You always. . . .
M: Well, sometimes.

(Cut short the typical mother/son interchange and keep them focused on the task. Don't let the son divert you into a discussion about the fairness of the chores.)

C: Does John want to do these chores?
M: No.
C: What makes the difference between the times he does them and the times he doesn't?
M: I guess it depends on whether he feels like it.

(Mom still believes that she can get John to do something only if he is self-motivated. You, as the counselor, must get Mom to see that she is successful, even when John doesn't want to do something.)

S: No way. It's when Dad and you get on my case.

(The son, probably unknowingly, comes to the rescue.)

M: Well, Dad can make him do it the first time. Me, it takes ten times.

(Here, the counselor wants to explore both areas: how dad is successful on the first time, and how Mom is successful on the tenth.)

C: What does Dad do on the first time?
M: He tells him to do it *NOW*.
C: Does that work?
M: Yes, for the most part.
C: What makes the difference between your first unsuccessful time and your tenth successful time?
S: She means it.

(Son comes to the rescue again.)

C: What do you mean, John?
S: I don't know; she just means it. I can just tell.
C: (to mother) How do you mean it on the tenth time, Mom?
M: I'm usually so angry by then, I just tell him to take out the garbage right now. I mean *NOW*. 'Here let me help you get started.'
C: When you tell him clearly and specifically, 'Take out the garbage now' I mean it,' you are successful, and he takes out the garbage?
M: Yes, but I don't like having to get so angry at him to get him to do it. I hate nagging.

(Reasonable argument and, interestingly enough, structurally similiar to the father's. He doesn't want to get angry or nag like his dad did with him because he loves his son.)

C: Well, the anger is a side-effect of nine frustrating attempts. I'm sure that if you said in the same clear, specific manner, 'Take out the garbage now. Here, let me help you get started,' and meant it on the first time, you could get him to do it without your getting angry.
M: Yes, but I hate having to tell him over and over again.
C: Yes, but he has learned that you don't mean it the first nine times and that if he pushes long enough, he can probably get out of doing the work.
M: But that sounds like I'm going to become like Hitler and tell him what to do and when. He is sixteen years old, and he needs to make some decisions on his own.
C: I agree. You don't want to make all of his decisions for him or become dictatorial. But are school grades and attendance negotiable issues? Are you willing to let him make this particular decision?

(The mother's arguments in the last few interchanges seem reasonable; however, her reasons need to be both challenged and supported. Point out to her, if you need to, that in this particular situation her reasonableness has contributed to the problem. Keep in mind that her need to be reasonable may also involve transgenerational issues which up to this point have not been explored. Some counselors might see these last interchanges as resistance on the mother's part. Again, I saw them as legitimate, reasonable questions and concerns until proven otherwise. If the interventions work then there is no problem. If they do not work, then there is a problem, and you need to reconsider the more complex "family dynamics". Start simple, then go complex.)

M: No. He has to go to school and get good grades. No choice.
F: I see what you're getting at. When issues are important to us, we have to give clear messages about them; we have to mean what we say and make things happen if they are not happening on their own.

Step Five: Summary of Information and Comparison of Successful vs. Unsuccessful Techniques

C: That's right. Whenever you as parents decide that something is really going to happen, and you clearly tell John to do it, he does it, even if he doesn't want to. When you mean what you say, when you give him no choice, and, if need be, help him get started on the task, then you are both very successful at getting him to do what you want him to do. (Make explicit the parents' successes. Reiterate some of the actual examples they gave to you in Step Four.) For example, today you mentioned that you got him to come to this counseling session, even though he didn't want to come; you got him to do his chores when he knew you meant it; you got him to abide by your restrictions; and I am sure that if we explored other areas, there would be many more times that both of you were successful at getting him to do what you wanted.

Yet, when it comes to going to school, staying in school, and getting straight C's, because you believed that he should know better; that he should make the decision himself; that he was possibly hyperactive; that he was bored with school; that boys will be boys; that Dad was gone a lot; or, that you, Dad, didn't want to be unreasonable like your father, you communicated with him differently and used completely different back-up techniques and principles. (Again, reiterate parental beliefs and actual examples of communication and interaction patterns.) Under these conditions, you actually said . . . (give examples), which gives him the choice to go to school or not, as long as he is willing to take the punishment. Also, because you have been so reasonable as parents, he realized that even if you restricted him or punished him, that he could probably get out of some of it for good behavior. More importantly however, in this goal behavior of going to school and getting at least C's, you never told him concretely and specifically what he must do—go to school, stay in school and get straight C's. This type of indirect, vague, abstract interaction with your son has been reasonable based on your belief systems, but now you can see that those beliefs do not have objective evidence to substantiate them. Now, if you wish, you can use some of the same concrete, clear communication-patterns and back-up techniques you have used in the areas where you have been successful with your son, in the areas where you are having difficulty with him.

M: Yeah. I see that, and it makes sense to me. But what do you do when he doesn't get the C's?

(This comment may be interpreted from many different perspectives: (1) she is, again, resistant; (2) she is setting the counselor up to seem incompetent; (3) she sees the situation as hopeless; or (4) she really wants to know. Until proven otherwise, I always operate under the assumption that parents who ask a question want to know. Don't tell them what to do, but give them the information which they need so that they can be successful. If you give them the information, and the intervention doesn't work, then that tells you there is something else going on and you need to drop back and re-evaluate the situation.)

C: What would be a clear message to John that you love him so much that you will not allow him to be unsuccessful, that he must get straight C's, and that there is no way out of this?

M: Make him do his school work when I tell him to.
C: Yes, that's right. You don't have to label him as "lazy" or "stupid", or lecture him about how important education is; he already knows that. He is very smart and capable; he knows. The point is, get him to do the work, and you won't have to punish him for not doing it. Tell him once exactly what he must do, and then back it up with some behavior that says, "I mean it. You must do this now. Here, let me help you get started right now." This same principle or idea is an example of what you did so successfully to get him to come to this counseling session and to do his chores at home.
M: I understand the principles, but what do I do when he doesn't get C's? You know he doesn't bring his books home. He says that his teachers don't give any homework. We've tried progress reports, and he loses them.

(At this point you must be careful not to tell the parents what to do. They must make the decisions and be willing to follow through. They are aware that they are successful in many different areas without the help of a counselor. Therefore, if the parents really wish their son to be successful now that they understand the principles behind their success, they can get him to do it. However, sometimes it is necessary to illustrate to parents some expedient back-up techniques that other families have used. Why make parents struggle to find an answer if a few simple examples are all that is necessary? Demonstrate the principle of back-up techniques with examples. If they copy your examples, just make sure that they take the credit for the success. If they come up with their own creative back-ups, that's even better. If they don't follow through, that tells you that something else is going on, and in later sessions you should explore more for hidden agendas and payoffs for the student's continued problems.)

C: Each family is different, and they all come up with creative ways of backing up their demands without punishing the child. I already know that both of you are very successful at getting John to do certain things that he doesn't want to do when you mean it and think that it is reasonable and important. Also, I know that there are many other areas in which you are successful which we have not explored. However, to illustrate a non-punishing

back-up technique in the school homework area, I'll share with you one way another family handled a similiar situation. (I tell them the long story of the parents staying up until 3:30 to make their son do his homework. See example in *How to Deal with Discipline Problems in the Schools,* Chapter VI, pp. 116-119.)
M: I get it.
F: I see what you are saying.

Step Six: Checking the Parents' Perceptions of What Has Transpired

C: Great, why don't you tell me in your own words what you've learned from this session today.

(In other cases, this step can serve as a check for misunderstandings and possible child abuse. However, most parents, by this time, understand the method and, if there are no major problems in the family, they know what to do to be successful.)

F: Say what you mean, and mean what you say!
C: Yes, and if the issue is important and non-negotiable, back up your demand.
M: Yes. Back it up, not with threats and punishment, but with just making him do what he needs to.
C: You're right. You're showing him that you care and love him so much that you will not let him be a failure. Although the principles sound simple, you understand that following through is not always easy. If John tests you, you must be emotionally prepared to commit yourself 100% to make sure he is successful and prove to him that you love him and will not let him be a failure.
F: Yes, we know that.
C: If you decide to work on this and then back off, John will know that if he puts up enough of a stink, he will not have to do his school work and more importantly he will know you don't love him enough to make sure he is successful.

(This statement forces the parents to make a stand and clearly state if they love the boy, and if they are willing to be parents and make it work.)

F: Yes, we understand that, and we aren't going to back off because we do love him and want him to be successful.

C: Great. It sounds like you have the idea. Here is a summary handout (see copy in Appendix C) that has some helpful information that other families have found useful. Let's plan to get together in two weeks for a follow-up session here at school. However, I'll call in a week to see how things are going and see if we really need to get together again. John is a neat young man, and I doubt you will have any trouble getting him back on track. However, if you have any questions or problems, or if John is not doing well in school, please don't wait for the two weeks; feel free to call me right away.

F: We will.

Step Seven: Practice and Role Play

In extreme cases, it may be necessary to have the family demonstrate what they plan to do if the problem arises. If so, have them develop a behavioral intervention plan that spells out exactly what they want to say and do if a problem comes up. (This is very similar to the teachers' individualized discipline lesson plan.) In this particular case, this step was not necessary. (You will find a guide for parental intervention plans in Appendix B.)

Chapter VI: Cases

In this chapter, I will present summaries of other cases so you can get a broader perspective of this approach and see how it can be used with various problems.

The Parents Who Couldn't Agree

A sixteen-year-old girl was referred to me by a high-school counselor because she was truant from school, failing most of her classes, and beginning to show a lot of negative behavior at school. The father was called at work, and he agreed to bring the family in for a counseling session. These upper-middle-class parents had two children, a nineteen-year-old son in the military service and this sixteen-year-old daughter. There were no significant extended family members living in the area or involved with this particular problem.

During the early socialization phase, the talk was light, energetic, and full of good-natured fun and laughter. My initial feeling was that this would be a family with which I would enjoy working.

The mother and daughter sat close to each other, and the father moved his chair a slight distance away, turning to face them. (Sometimes the seating arrangement gives you some clues to the family structure.) As we settled down to Step One of the model, setting the goal, it became apparent that the parents differed philosophically about their daughter's upbringing.

When asked what the problem was, the father took the lead and indicated that the daughter was truant from school a lot and was failing most of her classes. When asked how that was a problem to him, he indicated that it really bothered him, and he wanted his daughter back in school being successful. The mother was asked if it was a problem to her and if she agreed with the father that it was a problem. She indicated that it was not as much of a problem to her as to her husband. In fact, on a few occasions when the daughter missed school, they would go shopping and have lunch together "out on the town".

In essence, the father felt that the mother was too lax and let the daughter get away with too much while the mother felt that the father was too structured and rigid. She felt he was "always on her case and expected too much from her."

Many times communication within a family is symbolic and conveys meaning on several different levels. In this particular situation, the mother seemed to be talking for both the daughter and herself. As we continued the family session, it became clear that the daughter was getting two different messages from the parents. Because of the family's honesty and friendliness, I decided to use a rather dramatic technique to see if I could get the parents, for the sake of the daughter, to agree on what would be appropriate school behavior.

I turned to the daughter and told her to leave the session immediately. The daughter looked perplexed but started to get up and leave. As she got up, I told her in a rather stern voice, "Sit down and don't get up until I tell you to." As she sat down, I told her to get up and leave the room immediately. The family was startled by this maneuver. I quickly asked the daughter how she felt, and she admitted that she was "a little confused." She indicated that she was not sure what I was expecting. I turned to the parents and said, "Your daughter has been getting two different messages. One is, 'Go to school and get good grades' and the other is, 'It's okay to miss school and not get A's and B's.' There is nothing wrong with either message; each is probably backed up by legitimate reasons or beliefs about how to raise children. The problem is, however, that they are competing with each other and confusing your daughter. She does not know what you are really saying or expecting from her." (I relabeled the daughter as a "confused kid"; she had been labeled more negatively by both the school and the parents.)

Besides being generally confused about what the parents wanted, the daughter cared about them and loved them and she knew that no matter which message she followed, she would hurt one parent. I then asked the daughter to move her chair so that she would be sitting next to me (a symbolic physical relocation to move her out from between the parents). Then I directed the parents to turn their chairs toward each other, move closer together and discuss the situation, deciding on a solution to the problem. (This was a maneuver designed to try to clarify the parent/child boundaries and help the parents, as a team, to make a stand and set limits in relation to their daughter's school behavior and performance.) I then told the parents that they must come to some agreement on the message which they wish to give to their daughter and be willing to support each other. I emphasized the importance of this task by telling the parents that the daughter was a neat person, not a trouble-maker, and I was convinced that she was just nervous and confused about what to do and whose direction to follow. I told them that as soon as they came to an agreement, I was sure that the school's problems could probably be solved very quickly.

Then I turned to the daughter and said, "This is very important. You're old enough to know and understand complexities of human relations. Watch and learn from your parents trying to deal with a very difficult situation, so later when you are in adult relationships you will have a better understanding of how to deal with important issues."

I instructed the parents to discuss the issues and come to an agreement. They made a few polite attempts to define the problem the way each of them saw it, then both laughed and said the problem was that they couldn't agree on what to do. I indicated to them that I understood that it was very difficult to come to an agreement but they needed to do so if the daughter's school-related difficulties were to be solved.

The parents looked at each other as if they were seeking a non-verbal consensus or permission to speak. The father then said, "I don't really think we can come to an agreement. We are like night and day, so much so that we have decided to get a divorce." I asked the parents if they had talked this over openly with their daughter, and they indicated they had not. They weren't sure how to go about it, although they felt that she knew something was up because things had been building up to this over the past few years. I agreed with them that at some level she probably did know that there was something wrong, and the fact that it had not been openly discussed with her may have contributed to her confusion and anxiety. I told the parents that I thought it was extremely important for them to sit down and honestly discuss their plans with their daughter.

I realized that the school's problems were not the family's number-one priority at this time. However, the family's problems were beyond the scope of the school. I referred the family to counselors in private practice and tried tactfully to re-focus the issue to the daughter's educational needs. My rationale was to provide the daughter with parental clarity, structure, and support in her school-related difficulties in the hope that doing so would clear up some issues about where she fits in this new family constellation, and knowing her place would indirectly help her to deal with other pending family problems.

After being empathetic and supportive of all the members of the family, I asked the parents, "Even if you have personal differences and have agreed to divorce, which is understandably hard on everyone, is it okay if your daughter continues to act as she has been? Even though you are getting a divorce as husband and wife, is there anything you can do as a team to help her with her education?"

There was a long pause, then a few general comments from the parents indicating that they weren't sure if there was much they could do or agree on. I asked them whether their daughter's education was important to them, and if they were willing to work together to help her. They both agreed that her education was important, but they differed on how to help her. I asked them, "If you get a divorce, are you planning on divorcing yourselves from your daughter and her needs to be parented?" They again both strongly agreed that they loved their daughter and were not divorcing themselves from her. They indicated that they really had many things to work out and were not sure how this education issue was going to be resolved. I carefully asked the parents how sure they were that they were going to get a divorce; they indicated in a friendly but firm way that they were sure.

Based on the fact that they couldn't agree on what to do about their daughter's education, and that they were sure they were getting a divorce, I then told the parents that part of the outcome of the daughter's education appeared to be contingent on which parent the daughter would live with. I asked if they had decided which parent she would live with, and they said they had not decided on that issue either.

At this point there was no reason to continue the counseling session. It was clear that there was a lot of work to be done and that there was not going to be any solution reached in this school-based session. In a supportive way, I made it clear that the family had some major issues which they needed to talk over, clarify, and resolve. I suggested that the daughter was perceptive and knew something was going on within the family but that lack of information was making her very anxious. I told the parents that they needed to start making some decisions, and where appropriate, include the daughter in family discussions or at least keep her informed on what was happening so she wouldn't worry. I strongly recommended that they seek private counseling to: (1) help them resolve some of the issues that were going on between them; (2) help them resolve some of the parenting issues in relation to their daughter; and (3) help and support the daughter through this time of transition.

I ended the session with supportive statements to the family and an indication to the daughter that even though the school personnel could not support her inappropriate behavior, they cared about her. I told her that if at any time she needed someone to talk to, either the school counselor or I would be available to her. I indicated that I understood she might be going through some hard times, as well as her parents, but as a school staff, we would not tolerate any inappropriate behavior on her part. I assured her that we cared, but that she could also count on us to take an active stance to help her through school because we felt that it was important.

I also indicated that we understood some of the worry, anger, pain, and mixed-up, confusing feelings that might emerge during this period of transition. I said that I saw her as a very capable, competent, young woman who was hurting but who, I felt, had the strength and courage to face the hurt and deal with it, even though it would be painful. I also let the daughter know that we would be glad to work with her to try to help her understand and channel those feelings in a more positive direction.

High-School Student Staying at Home: A One-person Model vs. A System's Approach

I had a referral from a counselor to work with a female high school student who was being truant from school. I called the mother and asked her to come in for a family-counseling session. Since the father was deceased, the mother and daughter came to the session alone. After preliminary socialization, we began exploring the goals for the session, analyzing the beliefs, and going through the remaining steps of the model. The goals were never clearly stated because the mother never really believed that the daughter could consistently go to school and stay in school. I asked why she believed that her daughter couldn't go to school on a consistent basis. She went through quite a few beliefs. She felt that the daughter might be too sensitive and incapable of dealing with the hurts and cruelties inflicted by unkind students at school. I tried to erode those beliefs by asking what evidence she had to support this contention. I questioned, challenged, and debated them with the mother. I even questioned transgenerational issues and asked the mother if she ever had people say cruel things to her when she was in school and she indicated that she had. I asked if her parents allowed her to leave school and she said, "Oh no, I had to stay there in school. My parents wouldn't let me come home."

I asked, "If your parents didn't let you come home, why do you let your daughter come home? It seems like the same type of things happened to you, to me, and to everybody else that I know of. Some people say cruel things; why do you think your daughter is incapable of dealing with this problem?" We continued exploring these issues without any resolution.

I finally thought that maybe I was missing something important here and perhaps the deceased father had something to do with the problem. I explored some issues about the father but found no clear indication that his memory, influence, or beliefs had anything to do with the problem. Although, the daughter had to do some of the nursing care for her dying father, she seemed to have no apparent hidden or negative feelings that might be influencing the present problems. I then asked about other brothers and sisters. There was a younger, twelve-year-old brother in the family. He also stayed home. As I asked them why the brother stayed home, a significant look passed between the two. After some prodding, the mother said that her son was dying of cancer. At this point it became very clear what was happening.

From a family-systems life-cycle perspective, in this family there was a seventeen or eighteen year old daughter who was just about ready to leave home and go out on her own. The father had left the family through death. The younger brother was dying and would be leaving the family picture. The mother was the one, so to speak, left holding the bag, feeling the pressure and the hurt, and most definitely at high risk of falling apart. Many unresolved issues remained within the family. The problem wasn't just the daughter's being truant from school, it was the family context and the reality surrounding the behavior.

The mother indicated that her son didn't know about his impending death and that this was the big family secret. The daughter had to stay home and nurse the dying brother. I gave them some referrals and strongly suggested that they follow through and receive support for everyone in the family. I also suggested that on some level the boy probably knew how things stood. It might be a good idea to talk openly to him about it. From my perspective, the mother was justified in allowing her daughter to stay home and take care of her brother because it was a necessity at the time. I could have worked with that situation and would have loved to have worked with her to figure out some support systems to help the daughter and the family. But the mother persisted in saying that the daughter was weak, sensitive, and disturbed and couldn't deal with all these things that were going on. These statements by the mother disturbed me, more than the fact that the girl wasn't going to school. I gently tried to challenge and erode those beliefs, hoping that the mother would be able to take a more realistic perspective and say to the daughter that she needed her to stay home, rather than seeing and labeling her daughter in such negative terms.

At the close of the session, however, the mother said, "Well you know, none of this stuff is going to work." When I asked her why she believed that none of the interventions would work, she went right back to labeling her daughter as sensitive and unable to withstand the cruelty of other students. At this point I knew the interventions that I had suggested were not going to work.

Since the family had other more important issues to deal with, and I was unable to completely understand or erode the mother's perspective in the short time I had to work with her in the school setting, I tried to soften my and the school's position. I gave the mother other outside referrals for help. Still I indicated to the mother that her message to her daughter was clear: anytime anyone said or did anything that could be construed as cruel or hurtful, the girl had her permission to go home and stay home. I also indicated that it appeared to me that, under the circumstances, it was reasonable for the daughter to stay home, but not because she couldn't deal with other students. The session finished on an unresolved note.

At a follow up session, I met with the daughter on an individual basis. I let her know that I was concerned about what was said and done in the previous session, and that I wanted to cover any unfinished business. I told her that I cared about her and that I didn't want to cause her any more pain. I asked if she was upset with some of the things that were said by her mother or me in the previous session. I asked her how she felt about the previous session, and what she had been thinking about.

She sat back and thought for awhile and then said, "No, it was okay." Then she began to open up and we talked for about two more hours. She talked about how she used to see herself as an emotional, shy, sensitive person who couldn't deal with situations, the weak one in the family. She indicated, however, that the session made her do a lot of thinking. The attempt to erode the mother's belief systems, even though it was not successful, had allowed the daughter to question and erode her own beliefs about herself, and allowed her to begin to see herself in a more positive way. Rather than seeing herself as the shy, sensitive person who couldn't deal with situations, she had begun to see herself as the stronger one in the family. As support for this position, she indicated that she was the one who had to nurse and take care of her father when he was dying, and now she was taking care of her brother. She felt that her mother couldn't deal realistically with these issues. She said that she tried to talk to her mother on several occasions about her brother, but her mother couldn't deal with the situation and seemed to be falling apart. The daughter had some very good insights and began to talk about how she was caught in a bind. If she did start going back to school on a continuous basis, her mom would fall apart and she would be abandoning her brother. On the other hand, staying home jeopardized her schooling, her future college career, and some of her personal freedom. She said that she was willing to pay the price and sacrifice for a year or so just to get things stabilized within the family. She had understanding and insight and the rest of the individual session was very moving and sad. And yet, at a different level, it was very awe-inspiring to watch this young person face obstacles with such courage, inner strength and hope. Although it seemed that both the family and the individual session did not achieve the school's goal, I felt that, in a way, the session was successful because the daughter was able to see herself in a different light, and she was also at peace with herself and the decisions she had made. She changed even though the symptom of "being absent from school" did not change; she changed because her self-concept changed.

This particular case illustrates the broader context that a family-systems perspective provides the school counselor. It illustrates one of the benefits of working from a three-person systems approach rather than from a one-person model. It also points out how the counselor can help to change a person's internal, phenomenological perspective without necessarily changing the presenting problem behavior. Any other method which the school system might have employed to change the student's presenting behavior (behavior modification, for example) probably would not have changed the daughter's behavior either, and, more than likely, it would also have had an added disadvantage in that it would not have changed the subjective labeling process which the daughter was using on herself.

Pooping in the Pants—Two Different Outcomes

These two cases of school-aged youngsters defacating in their pants illustrate the effects of two different intervention structures with two different outcomes. One case was handled by another school psycholgist in the district and the other case by me.

I was new to this particular elementary school, and the administrator and staff were not aware of the approach I used. I was introduced to the principal, who then escorted me around the school introducing me to the teachers. One teacher indicated that she might need quite a bit of help and follow-up from me since she had four or five extreme cases that she would be sending referrals on. She told me about a particular student who was "going to the bathroom" in his pants.

My basic approach is that there is no problem until there is a problem. So I asked the teacher if this behavior was a problem to her. This first/second grade combination teacher said that she had quite a few years of experience with "poopers" and could handle the situation. She said that the mother brought a bag of extra clothing to school, so if the child pooped in his pants, the teacher would just change his clothes, put the soiled clothes into the bag, and deliver the bag to his mother. Listening to this, I was thinking that if I were the teacher I wouldn't tolerate the situation. I felt that the school was letting the child maintain his symptom. The principal quickly interjected, "Yes, we want to be very supportive of the parents. They are getting a lot of outside professional assistance and are seeing a psychiatrist." I interpreted that comment to mean, "as a school psychologist, don't interfere with the psychiatrist's role."

I figured that if the behavior was no problem to the teacher or to the principal, it was no problem to me. So I left the case completely alone and did not work with the family. What was interesting to me, however, was the longitudinal development of the symptom. When the child was in kindergarten, he never pooped in his pants—a clear indication of his capabilities. In first grade he started pooping in his pants, but not at school. He always pooped in his pants while walking the two blocks home from school. All the extra clothes and bags were sent to school "just in case". The fact that he never pooped in his pants in school and always did so on his way home also indicates extreme control, especially if he had to go to the bathroom at eight o'clock in the morning.

Interestingly enough, when I talked about this case to one of my colleagues (one who was not trained in this particular method), he mentioned that he had a similar case but with a different outcome. He said that he and the teacher couldn't, and wouldn't, put up with this type of behavior. They thought that it was inappropriate behavior and too much of an imposition on them, so they called the father at work, told him to come down and change the student's pants, and to tell the student not to do it again. The father did, and they never had another problem with it again.

Here are two similar problems with two different intervention philosophies or structures and, regardless of the possible dynamics of each case, two different outcomes.

Don't Bring Your Guitar or Don't Bring Your Marijuana

This case presented a role conflict for me. I wasn't the counselor, but I was in a quasi-administrative role in which I was required to be the heavy. The principal of a continuation high school with a very small staff was off campus for a meeting, and I was the acting administrator in his absence. The principal had forgotten to inform me that he had set up a parent meeting on a discipline case. A freshman girl along with several other students had gone over the back fence of the school and down into a drainage-ditch tunnel near the school. Once there, she played her guitar, sang, and smoked marijuana with the other students. She had been caught. Even though I had to operate from the school administrator's position, I wanted to offer some services to the mother in case she wanted back-up help to stop this type of behavior.

When the mother walked into the office, she hugged her daughter as though they were long lost friends and then sat down. Since I didn't know exactly why they were there, I questioned the mother as to the reason and told them why I was involved. When I asked the mother a question, the daughter answered for her. I asked the mother another question, and again the daughter answered. So I turned to the mother and asked her if it was all right for her daughter to speak for her and answer her questions. She said that it was okay, that it was interesting to see what her daughter's thoughts and perspectives were. I turned my chair around, faced the daughter, and talked to her for awhile to see what the problem was in terms of being truant, playing the guitar, and smoking marijuana.

As we went through the conference, I felt caught between roles. I didn't want to be the school heavy, and I didn't want to get into a family-counseling session under these circumstances. However, an interesting thing happened when we were winding up the session. I asked the mother if she would be interested in letting her daughter know what she expected from her in terms of her behavior at school. The mother emphatically told the daughter never to bring her guitar to school again. She said nothing about smoking marijuana or leaving the campus. The daughter never did bring the guitar to school again, but she continued to smoke and leave campus.

Excerpts from Cases of Parents Who Lie to Their Children

Many parents who are having difficulties with their children don't trust them and believe that the only way they can get them to do anything is to hide the truth from them, manipulate them, or lie to them. In private practice, parents have come to my office and as I'm exploring Step Four of the therapy model (how the parents have been successful at getting their child to do what they want him to do, even though the child didn't want to do it), I've asked them, "How did you get him to come to this office? He's seventeen years old, and so far it sounds like he's not interested in being here. How did you get him to come here?" Usually, the parents just say something like, "Well, I just told him he had to come; he had no choice in the matter; we just brought him." That's the usual response, and that's what I'm looking for.

In one particular case, however, the mother and father looked at each other, looked at their son, and then said that they had told him they were going to dinner. The message to the youngster is that the parents really don't trust him and can't tell him the truth. It also becomes clear that he can't trust the parents either. I asked the parents, "Why do you believe your son is such a wishy-washy, spineless individual that he can't deal with reality? Why do you believe you can't tell him, honestly, that you're going to see a psychologist? Why do you feel you have to lie to him?" Counselors and psychologists need to confront the parents and explore these particular belief-systems in the session to get the family to be more open and honest with each other.

I gave this example at a seminar for nurses. Afterwards, one nurse told me of a family who had brought their daughter into the hospital for a tonsillectomy. When the little girl came out of recovery, she began to cry. She cried and cried. The nursing staff tried everything they could think of to get the little girl to calm down, but they just could not get her to stop crying. Finally, after questioning the parents, they found that the girl's parents had told their daughter that they were just going out to get some ice cream.

Both of these cases illustrate why some children get a little anxious when their parents say they are going someplace. Even though the results may be tragic, the parents are usually not motivated by malice. Sometimes the motivation stems from wanting to "protect the child from the hurts of the world." My experience has shown that children can deal with hurtful, complex, or sometimes scary things if parents are honest with them and tell them the truth in a context of love, caring, and courage. I believe that it is much better to be honest with your children than to lie to them.

I've had variations of this phenomenon when working with delinquent and pre-delinquent populations. The parents would say, "We're so exasperated we're ready to kill this kid." I'd ask them what they said or did to correct the problem and the conversation would go something like this:

Parent: Well, I told him if he did it again I'd take him down to juvenile hall and have him locked up.
Counselor: Did he do it again?
Parent: Well yes, he did it again. That's why we are still having the problem and why we are here to see you.
Counselor: Did you take him to juvenile hall and lock him up?
Parent: No. What kind of parents do you think we are?
Counselor: Basically, you are lying to your child, probably for very legitimate reasons. However, the fact still remains, you are not saying what you really mean, and to add to that, you are not following through.

Naturally, you don't want the parents to lock up their child; you don't even want to give the parents that choice. The point is, the student knows that the parents make these threats without intending to follow through.

This type of message really leads to a sense of insecurity in the student. I believe that a variety of "neurotic" behaviors appear because the student doesn't really know where he fits in or what's going on in the family. If the parents lie about taking their child to dinner, the next time they mention taking him to dinner, he may exhibit rather bizarre behaviors. This type of situation reminds me of Rodney Dangerfield saying that he went to school one day, and when he came home his parents had moved. One does tend to become a little insecure.

If the student doesn't know where his place is in the family, it is almost a guaranteed corollary that he is not secure in his relationships with others, and he is not sure about whom to trust. This same type of "acting-out insecurity" phenomenon happens in many divorce situations in which the child gets the message, "Keep that up and I'm sending you to your father's to live." Six months later while living with the father, the child hears, "Keep that up and I'm sending you back to your mother." Some children don't know where they "really" fit in and whom they can count on, both within and out of the family.

Different Parental Expectations

This is an example of toilet-training a male child, approximately two-and-a-half years of age, at a time when the child's parents were going through a divorce. When the child lived with his father he was basically toilet-trained, but when he lived with his mother he was not. According to the court's reconciliation counselor, this inconsistent behavior occurred because of the mother's belief-system that boys developed later than girls, and therefore she couldn't expect the child to be toilet-trained. Even though there is some truth to this belief, observe the outcome in terms of demonstrated behavior. During their reconciliation counseling, the parents transferred the child back and forth between themselves every couple of weeks. The father didn't want to deal with changing diapers and made the child go to the bathroom in the toilet. The mother, because of her belief in the later development of boys, did not expect her child to be toilet-trained for another six months or so. Note that because of each parent's underlying belief-system, whether founded on fact or not, different parental expectations for this child obtained different behavioral outcomes.

A Thumbsucker

A high-school teacher had a young child who kept sucking his thumb. He had tried everything, including spankings, awful-tasting ointments, and bandaging the thumb. After hearing one of my presentations, he decided to give his child a clear message not to suck his thumb anymore. He looked the child straight in the eye and told him, "*Never* suck your thumb again." He said his son started to put his thumb toward his mouth but then changed to his index finger, stuck that in his mouth and started sucking it. This child is what might be called a "loophole, concrete thinker".

School Phobic

This is a case of a seventh-grade student who was supposedly "school phobic". Initially, the student would go to school, vomit and have the school nurse send him home. His mother had him thoroughly examined by a doctor to find that there was nothing physically wrong with him. The doctor gave the mother a referral and suggested that his problems were psychological.

By the time I became involved in the case, the student had spent six months in therapy with a behavioral therapist who was doing systematic approximations and reinforcements to get the student to go to school. The general plan was something like this: First, the student would take a few steps out of the home, next he would start down the walk towards school with his mom, then without his mom, and finally he would try a few steps alone. After accomplishing this much, he would then progress in small increments until eventually he would go to school, stay there for a shortened day, and of course, eventually it was hoped that he would stay there for a full day. After six months of this therapy, at $75 an hour, the mother was frustrated. The child hadn't gotten very far, and she was in jeopardy of having her second marriage fail.

I worked with the mother and took an active, firm stance to find out what she wanted her son to do. She wanted him to get back into school. I told her to bring him to school, make him stay, give him a clear message to make it happen—don't give him any choice. I suggested that she must do whatever it takes to make this happen. The mother said she wasn't sure she could do it on her own. Her husband was a trucker and gone a lot, and the boy was starting to come between them. Her husband had indicated that if she didn't get this problem under control, and get the child back in school, he might leave. The mother said that her husband was a good man and that she loved him and wanted to stay with him. I said, "Fine, then make the child go to school. If you can't use your husband because he is gone, then ask some neighbors, friends, or hire a football player to help you get your son to school and keep him there." She decided she'd try it on her own. I asked if she needed any help dealing with the "throwing up" issue.

"No," she said, "I'll just tell the school nurse, 'if he throws up, tough. Tell him he has to clean up the mess himself. He's staying in school and he is *not* coming home'."

She also included some general rules that she was going to enforce around the home. She told her son that she loved him, could spend only so much time with him, and would not let him come between her husband and herself any longer. He was not going to ruin her marriage; she was married and was going to stay married. She set down some very clear rules, and was very pleased that it was okay to be a parent.

Interestingly enough, the child was back in school the next day. She escorted him to school, told him he could not miss any more school, and if he threw up, he could clean it up himself. She told him that he was to stay in school no matter what, that he was not to come home, and that she had informed the nurse and school authorities of her wishes. She had the child in school the next day, and he never missed another day of school for the rest of that year.

In some of these cases, there are other psychological and "quality of life" issues for the family, the parents, and the children involved that could be dealt with in counseling. The important thing is, if the family can solve the major presenting problem, then that is one less major problem which the student or the family has to deal with; in some cases this clears up many other issues and problems, or, at the very least, frees up some time and energy to deal more effectively with other issues. It is obvious to me that this "school phobic" and his family could still use some help, nevertheless, the student is in school, and the family can now choose to spend $75.00 an hour on therapy to deal with other quality-of-family-life issues. If the family or student still needs counseling, continue to work on the relevant emotional or personal growth issue, or refer them for outside professional help. But, regardless of all these other wide-ranging and more complex considerations, such as the child's self-concept and worth, the quality-of-life issues, the parents marital problems, and other psychological subtleties, do not let the student act inappropriately at school.

Chapter VII: Questions and Answers
BEHAVIOR MODIFICATION

Question: You often put down behavior modification. How do you account for its success?

Answer: I probably shouldn't talk so dogmatically about behavior modification because it does work with some children. There is no question about it. My feeling is, however, that when it does work, it works for reasons different from the ones usually given by behavior modifiers. I believe that you can change children's inappropriate behavior much easier and much quicker using other approaches, especially this one.

Again, my philosophy is, there is no problem until there is a problem. If behavior modification works for you, if it is expeditious, and if you like it, then there is no problem. Please use it.

I have no qualms about the principles of reinforcement for rewarding positive behaviors, and the acquisition and maintenance of those positive, social, appropriate behaviors. I just happen to call those types of deeds caring, loving, courtesy, politeness, manners, and education. Please give others all the "warm fuzzies" and positive strokes you can. It makes the world a better place.

The area in which I personally have the most trouble with behavior modification, even though I know that it works, is initially stopping inappropriate behavior and working on successive approximations of those goals and behaviors. If anyone really stopped to think about it, he would realize that the child already knows how to do what he is supposed to do. In these areas, I guess I am too impatient and am unwilling to work for successive approximations of the final goal behavior, to take baselines and waste a lot of time trying to find the right reinforcers to get the child to stop the inappropriate behavior and be motivated enough to do what is desired. My feeling is that educational systems in the United States, for the most part, do not demand or expect too much behaviorally out of our children that is beyond their range of capability. In some ways, behaviorally, we expect more, and get more out of dogs than we do out of some children. And I am *absolutely* convinced that most children are more intelligent than most dogs and have the behavior repertoire and potential to act appropriately in school.

I mentioned earlier in this answer that I thought behavior modification worked for different reasons than the ones ususally given by behavior modifiers. Here are some alternative explanations.

Alternative Explanations for the Success of Behavior Modification

Even though behavior modification is frequently successful, it is my contention that it is not the behavior modification *per se,* or the scientific technology systematically applied, that accounts for the major portion of the behavioral change. In my view, at least four factors exist other than behavior modification technology that explain the majority of the change:

(1) Clarity: Knowing the Structure and Setting Clear Rules

For behavior modification to work, standards and rules must be set clearly and specifically. The parents, teacher, and child need to know what the contingencies are, which behaviors will be reinforced, and which behaviors will not be reinforced. Behaviors have to be described in very specific, concrete, observable terms so the adults using the system can tell which behaviors need to be reinforced and which need to be extinguished. When parents or other adults are made to clarify these issues, they not only set the behavioral standards and goals, but they also restructure the hierarchy of the family, and, in essence, place the adult back in a position of authority. The person setting the standards is the one who clarifies the structure and sets up a complementary relationship (*e.g.,* parent/child, teacher/student). The very fact that someone is in an authority position and is willing to set the standards, who then clarifies the behaviors to be reinforced and resets the system's hierarchy, I believe, accounts for a large portion of the change attributed to behavior modification.

All of a sudden, chaos has been given order. The student or child and the teachers or parents now know what the rules are and what is expected. They have a game-plan, a map. Not only have the system and the goals for both the parents and the child been clarified, but also another message has been given. That message is: The teachers or the parents are the ones making the decision, not the student or the child. Within that new structure the teachers or the parents make the decisions, and the student or child reacts to that structure. This process of setting and clarifying the standards, rules, and contingencies follows a family-systems maxim: Parents need to be parents, and children need to be children.

(2) Consistency

For behavior modification to work, there has to be consistency: goals must be clarified, standards set, and rules regularly enforced and reinforced. To be consistent, the adult has to get more involved with the child, watch him, and give him the proper reinforcements. Someone must be present to consistently monitor and reinforce the program.

If someone were to "say it and mean it" and follow through with consistent, effective back-ups, this, in and of itself, would more than likely account for the change, rather than all the charts, stars, trinkets, schedules, contracts, successive approximations and reinforcements of behavior modification. If someone is there giving the family or the classroom structure, if someone is there *being a parent or a teacher,* if someone sets the rules and consistently backs them up, then anything that you use—including behavior modification—works.

(3) Personal Involvement and Contact Closeness

The third element is related to what Dr. Jim Alexander from the University of Utah calls "contact closeness". In his model of Functional Family Therapy, Alexander postulates core "functions" of social interactions: People either get farther away from each other (distancing), closer together (contact closeness), or they like a mid-pointing position (not too close, not too far away). In order to have behavior modification work successfully, someone (mainly the teacher or parent) must be there observing, watching, reinforcing, and extinguishing certain behaviors. This person needs to be involved with the child, at least to watch the child, and then be there to hand out the trinkets, the stars, and any other primary or secondary reinforcements. All of this involvement engenders more contact with the child, more praise, and more closeness. Even if you use what Alexander calls mid-pointing techniques (close, but at the same time distant), such as saying, "I care about you, and love you indirectly through the use of stars and trinkets that I'm giving you," involvement and contact are increased. The parent or adult in charge has to be much more observant and involved with the child if the behavior-modification program is to work. This factor probably accounts for another large portion of the variance of change rather than just the technology of the behavior-modification approach.

(4) Paradoxical Directives

A fourth alternative explanation for behavior modification's success is that some of behavior modification's initial interventions are paradoxical. Many self-monitoring behavior modification approaches direct their clients to continue the behavior, but to write it down and get a baseline on that particular behavior; the client counts these behaviors to become aware of what's going on. Amazingly enough, behaviorists report that when people make their baselines over a period of time, the behavior diminishes just on that intervention alone. In a sense, that directive is paradoxical because it tells someone to do a particular behavior, only with a slight variation that the therapist controls—telling the client to mark down the behaviors on a sheet of paper to find the baseline. This fairly standard paradoxical technique, "do the behavior more, but under my direction, and in a slightly different way", is also used by many theorists. Most family therapists use similar paradoxical directives with equal success, but without the behavior-modification technology or paraphernalia.

SPECIAL EDUCATION

Question: What are some of your thoughts on special education and IEP's?

Answer: Historically, special education has, for the most part, been a very positive, important, and necessary force in reshaping education and in getting appropriate services for children with special needs. Recently, in the special-education field, some previously held assumptions are beginning to be challenged, especially those related to learning disabilities. I wish to address my comments about special education to the specific area of learning disabilities only.

I believe that we in education have "bought into" several assumptions or philosophical positions in relation to learning disabilities that really need to be questioned and challenged. Heading the list is the assumption that individualized instruction is best, and in order to get it the student needs to be placed in a special class. The belief that many students can learn only through individualized instruction in special classes has inadvertently undermined American education and will probably bankrupt it if it is continued. Although in many cases individual instruction is necessary, as a major educational philosophy it is disastrous, and it has been disastrous even in special education.

In special education the belief has been perpetuated that learning-disabled students must have individualized instruction, thereby suggesting that the student cannot learn unless he is in an individualized program. This idea, if internalized by educators, parents, and children, sets into motion self-fulfilling and self-defeating behaviors. Some parents have become convinced of this belief so strongly that they now demand and expect individualized instruction for their child, often at great expense to the school district. Because the parents believe that the student must have individualized instruction, and the student knows that the parents believe this, the student begins to believe that he cannot learn in regular classes. Eventually, if the student internalizes the belief, he acts accordingly, and the situation becomes self-fulfilling in a very negative way.

I'm always suspicious when I hear parents and students talk about how they absolutely need, and can't live without, individualized instruction. I realize that at times and in some places, individualized instruction is appropriate, but I want to know what evidence the parents or students have to substantiate their belief that the student can't control himself appropriately in a group or can't learn in regular education classes. I have seen capable though "learning disabled" students who fail when mainstreamed back into regular classes because they believed that they couldn't do the work. I've had parents tell their children, "See, I told you that you couldn't make it in regular-education class. You need those special classes to pass." I believe the meta message we give children by having them work at their own pace with individualized instruction, and the unforeseen consequences of placing children in learning-disabled programs, need to be weighed and seriously questioned in terms of the advantages and disadvantages.

I'm concerned about the toll which all of this takes on a student's self-concept over the years. It is tragic that most junior-high, senior-high, and even college-level learning-disabled students, when you get past the initial bravado and denial, really don't feel very good about themselves. They, for the most part, see themselves as being "dumb", "stupid", "lazy", or "crazy". and they usually act according to their self-definition. Even if you get them reading and functioning fairly well, they still, in many ways, see themselves in negative terms. Ask yourself, "How many of these children were emotionally disturbed when they entered school, and how many of them are now emotionally disturbing to the school?" I believe that most of this burden could be avoided with adequate, early intervention.

A corollary of the concept of individualized instruction is the belief that one has to work at his own pace and be self-motivated to want to do the work. I have seen special-education teachers use all kinds of "motivational techniques" and "reward systems" to get students to do ten to fifteen minutes of work per period—in some cases, per day, and, unfortunately, in some cases, per week. If you believe that you have to have the student work at his own pace (in most situations this means doing nothing), or believe that you have to wait until he wants to work, you're in deep trouble. (Review the examples in *How to Deal with Discipline Problems in the*

Schools, Chapter II and Chapter III, pages 45-47, 57-59, and the Helen Keller story, pp. 139-141.)

It is much more gratifying when students choose to want to work on their own, but the majority of special-education junior-high and high-school L.D. students whom I've worked with and observed don't choose to want to spend a lot of time on task—learning to read and write. Granted, it is absolutely imperative that you have good instructional techniques, a supportive educational environment, and good curriculum materials in place to help insure learning, but you can not just *sit* and *wait* and *hope* that the student will one day "see the light" and become self-motivated to do the work.

Special educators and parents need also to consider how labeling predisposes the student to continue the problem behavior. One mother told me her son was an "intermittent dyslexic". When I asked what she meant by the description, she replied that "his reading problem sort of comes and goes." She explained that at different times the child had certain "good" teachers and did very well. During those times the child didn't have dyslexia. There were other years when the child had "bad" teachers, and his problem worsened and he got further behind. I question the logic of labeling this student dyslexic, let alone "intermittent dyslexic".

This labeling process, as well as the desire to be accurate and correct about these labels, has brought on sophisticated diagnostic problems. Although identifying and labeling learning-disabled students has become a technically sophisticated skill, the essential question remains: Does any of this diagnostic sophistication give you any leverage to help the youngster solve his problems with reading, writing, or math? Does giving this particular youngster a label of Greek or Latin origin (dyslexic, dysgraphic, dyscalculic) help him do better in his schoolwork—or does it simply serve as a convenient "pseudo-scientific" explanation to gratify educators and parents?

Salvador Minuchin, a famous family therapist, once interviewed, for the benefit of the resident psychiatrists and psychologists who had come from all over the world to observe him doing his work and to receive training in his structural family therapy, a young woman who had an eating disorder. After he finished interviewing the girl and her family, he asked the psychologists and psychiatrists, "What seems to be the problem with this little girl?"

They replied, "Well, she's anorexic."

"No, no, no," he protested. "She's not anorexic; she's just not eating yet."

That simple story demonstrates that we can give pretentious labels to anything. So what! Does it help your understanding? Does it help the problem? Can you solve the problem of anorexia, or, is it easier to solve "not eating yet"? If any child is having problems reading, help him to read. It doesn't matter whether you refer to a student as "dyslexic" or just "a poor reader". Help him. How do you solve the problem of a learning disability once you've labeled it? The issue is that if someone can't read, work on that. If you can get him to read well, then there is no problem in that particular area. However, many students with reading problems, as well as their parents, get locked into these labels and the labeling process, thereby limiting the student for the rest of his life. To illustrate this point, consider this story of the elephant:

The elephant is the stongest "athlete" in the animal kingdom. But if you ever get backstage at a circus, you'll notice something very strange about the way trainers keep the elephants tied up.

Wrapped around the leg of the little baby elephant is a great big chain; but wrapped around the leg of the huge adult elephant is a little flimsy rope.

The elephant-trainer will tell you that after a few months of straining against a big chain, the baby elephant will finally give up. After that, the trainer can replace the big strong chain with a weak little rope, and the elephant never knows the difference. Even though the adult elephant could snap the rope with one mighty tug of his foot, he never even tries. Why? Because the long months of struggling against the chain have conditioned and convinced him to believe that it is impossible!

Very often, students, like the elephant, have been trained, conditioned, and labeled to believe and to limit their own potential. Like the elephant, if the student doesn't believe that he can read, or "break the rope", he won't.

Wilma Rudolph had a physically handicapping condition when she was young. However, she became the world's fastest woman runner and won numerous gold medals. If she is the fastest runner in the world, does she still need to label and conceptualize herself as physically handicapped? If a student who initially is a poor reader learns to read and write well, should he keep the label "learning disabled"? If he overcame the "disability", how did he do it? Did the new, refined, sophisticated Latin or Greek label of a "specific learning disability" magically solve the problem? My hunch is that if the student was successful, more than likely there was a lot of hard work done initially, and after much practice, and hopefully with the best educational techniques and instruction available, his performance became more fluent, autonomic, and done with less and less stress and frustration.

If a student doesn't read well initially, what does that student look like perceptually, neurologically, and/or psychologically, ten years down the line? If students are intelligent and verbal, how have they compensated for these learning difficulties over time? I hear experts say things like, "This student's preferred style of learning is 'a speaker/listener' ", as if that phrase explains something. I always like to ask, "What other choice does the student have if he can't read? If he doesn't know the sound/ symbol correspondence? If he doesn't know how to blend? How in the world could he choose to be 'a reader/writer'?" Do you think that if the student is smart, is a survivor, and he has to use his "speaker/listener" skills more and more to survive, that he might get better at it over time? That it might become autonomic and more of a "preferred" style of learning? I am sure that some of the same logic prevails in the visual- *vs.* auditory-preference debate.

My sense of all this is that out of the learning disabled students who have no organic visual or auditory difficulties, the students who have not learned the sound-to-symbol correspondence of the alphabet and do not know how to blend and sound words out, will be the students who develop some type or style of visual "preference". As a result, we will then have to develop more sophisticated diagnostic tests and instruments to detect the subtle differences in such students' preferred styles and modalities of learning. And, with all of this ever-increasing technical sophistication, the questions will remain, "Do we teach to the strength, or remediate the weakness?" "How do we get this student to learn how to read?"

I suspect that a lot of the students labeled "learning disabled" are not all that different in terms of differential diagnostic testing, preferred styles, or preferred modalities, from students in general who read or write poorly. The questions are: Is there that much difference between poor readers and learning disabled students, physiologically, perceptually, neurologically and psychologically? Could you really measure the differences with a WISC-R, WAIS-R, WRAT, Woodcock Johnson, Bender, or any other test? My initial assumptions are that most reading difficulties are the result of an instructional disability, a curriculum disability, a teacher disability, a school-philosophy disability, and/or a family interaction or structure disability, rather than a specific physiological, perceptual, or neurological disability that is so "easily" detected by these "technically sophisticated" instruments?

I suspect that the incidence of "learning disabilities" in this country would be greatly reduced if we could rule out these other possibilities for poor reading. As possible evidence for this contention, the incidence of illiteracy and learning or reading disabilities in Northern European countries is relatively low. Now it might be argued that they don't have the diagnostic sophistication, abilities, money, and resources that we have to meet these student needs; yet, some of the Scandinavian countries don't have as many reading difficulties, period. They don't need to have sophisticated differential diagnoses because the majority of students read well.

Phil McInnis, of New York, has instituted a specific instructional and curriculum-based reading program that has been implemented in a district for more than fifteen years. In that district they have reduced all their special-education referrals and placement from approximately 20% to less than 1%-3%. Their definition of being "behind" in reading is "five months below grade level, at any grade level", and any student in the district in that position can get remediational help. If this program continues to hold up under scrutiny, a lot of what we assumed to be "learning disabilities" may prove to be curriculum, instruction, and teacher disabilities.

As to the other portion of the question regarding IEP's, my feelings are that, generally, in the academic areas they can be helpful. However, if the curriculum is good and the teacher is very professional and knows her stuff, they are usually redundant and a waste of time. IEP's in the behavioral areas, I think, are a real waste of time, and furthermore, are at times even laughable. Look over the examples on the following pages and see what you think.

This is an actual IEP, which I copied from a California school district that I was in. This IEP is fairly typical of the IEPs that I have seen over the years.

The questions that I would like to ask are these:

Why let a student hit other students "one time per fifteen minutes"?

Why allow "one negative comment per ten minutes"?

Why wait until January or February to stop this behavior?

Why waste the time and energy to write all of this up, get baselines, set up contingencies, send the student to the counselor, and videotape all of this junk?

How did the S.A.T. committee come up with these magical numbers that it is okay to hit other students and give negative comments in the classroom?

All of these data and "solutions" are, to me, absurd. Do you realize that in a five-hour school day this means that this kid can hit other students twenty times a day, one hundred times a week, four hundred times a month, or four thousand times a year? This is, of course, only if the intervention program works. Otherwise, this student will hit others six times as much, or twenty-four thousand times a year. Either of these choices, to me, is professionally incomprehensible, and if I was a parent with a child on the other end of this student's hitting, I would use legal means to challenge the district for condoning such behavior.

The experience that ultimately convinced me that most of this I.E.P. stuff is a joke and a waste of time is the example of the new special-education teacher who in mid-year took over a self-contained classroom of extremely out-of-control, "emotionally handicapped" students. The IEPs for these twelve "acting-out" students were written in a similar fashion to the previous example: "By January there will be 85% less out-of-seat behavior as measured by...." To say the least, this new teacher came in like gang-busters. He did not put up with *any* inappropriate behavior in his classroom. He expected his students to behave right from the beginning, and, strangely enough, he got what he expected. It took hard work and he had

INDIVIDUALIZED EDUCATION PROGRAM (IEP)
Annual Goal/Short-Term Objectives

Annual Goal: Code #6.1
Description: Social Skills

Unified School District

Scott	6/25/71	Elementary	10/14/79
Individual's Name	D.O.B.	School of Attendance	IEP Meeting Date

Date Set	Present Level of Performance	ST Obj. Code # Desc.	SHORT-TERM OBJECTIVES (Must be time-referenced and include criteria for evaluation.)	Person Responsible	Date(s) Reviewed	Results (Indicate performance level.)	Met	Not Met
10/14/79	Hits other students an average of 6 times per 15-minute period on playground. (Observation data collected 9/17-9/23/79.)	6.1.1/A Interpersonal skills	By January 31, 1980, Scott will have reduced the number of times he hits other students on the playground an average of 1 time per 15 minutes, as measured by recorded observation counts conducted during 3 randomly selected 15-minute playground periods per week for 3 consecutive weeks.	L., L.H., Res. Specialist; and J., School Psychologist	1/31/80	Objective attained as stated.	x	
10/14/79	Makes an average of 5 negative comments per 10-minute period to others in the classroom. (Observation data collected 9/17-9/23/79.)	6.1.1/B Interpersonal skills	By February 20, 1980, Scott will make no more than (an average of) 1 negative comment per 10-minute period to others in the classroom, as measured by recorded observation counts conducted during 3 randomly selected 10-minute classroom periods per week for 4 consecutive weeks.	L. J.	2/10/80	Objective attained as stated.	x	62

IMPLEMENTATION/INSTRUCTIONAL PLAN (IIP)
Unified School District

Scott	6/25/71	L./J.	6.1
Individual's Name	D.O.B.	Person Responsible	Annual Goal Code No.

SHORT-TERM OBJECTIVE 6.1.1-A / By 1/31/80, Scott will have reduced the number of times that he hits other students on the playground to an average of 1 time per 15 minutes, as measured by recorded observation counts conducted during 3 randomly selected 15-minute playground periods per week for 3 consecutive weeks.

Code No. / Description

Date Set	Instructional Activities	Instructional Methods & Materials	EVALUATION Date(s) Reviewed	EVALUATION Results (indicate performance level)
11/08/79	Scott will identify "hitting behavior" by others on the playground.	—Observation/discussion —School counseling group	11/20/79	Attained as stated.
11/20/79	Scott will reduce hitting others to an average of 4 times per 15-minute period.	—Contingency management, with restrictive contingencies (e.g., exclusion from other students at recess) —Teach substitution behaviors —Role assignments (e.g., playground monitor) —School counseling group	12/15/79	Attained as stated.
12/15/79	Scott will reduce hitting others to an average of 2 times per 15-minute period.	—Same as above	1/10/80	Attained as stated.

IMPLEMENTATION/INSTRUCTIONAL PLAN (IIP)
Unified School District

Scott	6/25/71	L./J.	6.1
Individual's Name	D.O.B.	Person Responsible	Annual Goal Code No.

SHORT-TERM OBJECTIVE   6.1.1-B   /   By 2/20/80, Scott will make no more than (an average of) 1 negative comment per 10-minute period to others in the classroom, as measured by recorded observation counts conducted during 3 randomly selected 10-minute classroom periods per week for 4 consecutive weeks.

          Code No. / Description

Date Set	Instructional Activities	Instructional Methods & Materials	EVALUATION Date(s) Reviewed	Results (indicate performance level)
11/08/79	Scott will verbally identify from videotapes of himself and his classmates all negative comments made during class.	—Videotape —Discussion —School counseling group	12/10/79	Attained as stated.
12/10/79	Scott will reduce the number of negative comments made to others to an average of 3.5 per 10-minute period.	—Contingency management, with restrictive contingencies (*e.g.,* exclusion from other students in classroom) —Modeling (*e.g.,* positive comments) —Verbal reinforcement for positive comments monitor	1/25/80	Attained as stated.
1/25/80	Scott will reduce the number of negative comments made to others to an average of 2 times per 10-minute period.	—Same as above	2/05/80	Attained as stated.

to stay on top of the situation, but within less than one week that class was completely turned around. There was no fighting, hitting, cussing, or other inappropriate behavior. The students sat in their seats, raised their hands, and asked for permission to get up or speak in class. And, most amazingly, they started doing their work and turning in assigments.

I walked into this classroom about the third day to set up an appointment with the teacher to go over these elaborate IEPs because we had a state audit coming up that we needed to plan for. While there, I watched how this teacher effectively handled a discipline situation, and I thought to myself how absolutely stupid and asinine this paperwork is when you have a teacher who is committed to the belief that *there will be no inappropriate behavior* in his or her classroom—*period.* Why put up with, or condone any inappropriate behavior? Why wait until January or February just to get the behavior down to 40%? 50%? 60%? 85%?? Why not do everything you can *right now,* get the youngster under control, and make school a safe environment for everyone?

OTHER PROBLEMS

Question: How do you get parents to stop a student from swearing?

Answer: You can attack this problem from two basic angles. Depending on whether or not the student has a long history of swearing, the first angle might be more difficult—but it is one that should be incorporated into your total intervention plan.

First, you must tell the student clearly and specifically to "*stop* the swearing and to *never* swear again". You must have a real sense and belief that this new behavior *is* going to happen and that you *will not* tolerate any other option to this demand. If the child/student wishes to express himself in terms of his feelings, let him know that he can learn to do so in a more direct and appropriate way, a way other than by using inappropriate language. In rare situations you might have to incorporate some type of physical restraint, such as covering the child's mouth while simultaneously telling him to stop the swearing and never do it again.

Continue to back up this demand in this manner until the child gets the message that you mean business.

The second way to attack this problem is the primary intervention strategy of choice. Most children or students swear at their parents because they are upset or angry over some particular unresolved problem, such as truancy or poor grades. If the parents drop back one step and look at the issues about which the child is upset and then develop an intervention plan to solve those problems, most often the swearing at the parents will decrease. When the problem is solved, parents won't tend to "ride" the child about his inappropriate behavior because there is no longer any problem to deal with. When the student is doing well in school and is acting appropriately, he is less likely to become frustrated or angry about parental requests—or problems that don't exist. By the same token, when the student is doing well and there is no problem, parents are less likely to nag the student, and they are more likely to feel reasonably comfortable in allowing the student more freedom and privileges (using the car, trusting the student, staying out later, and so forth). The child has to get the message that the parents *will not* tolerate inappropriate behavior. Once the child understands that the parents are setting the standards and mean what they say, that there is *no other choice,* and that the parents are the parents and the child is the child, and that the problems or issues that everyone is upset about will be solved—*then* the swearing will usually stop.

Remember, as a secondary part to this primary intervention, you also need to tell the child that he is to "*stop* the swearing and is to *never* swear again". In terms of communication and quality-of-life issues within the family, you can say, "If you don't like some of the things that I am doing, and you wish to communicate to me in a way that indicates you would like to have some input into this decision-making process, here's how you can go about doing that. . . ." Then, teach the child some social skills; teach him what he needs to say and do rather than express himself in such inappropriate ways.

Question: A lot of times you don't talk to the student very much or ask how he feels about things. Why is that? Don't you think that you defeat some of your therapeutic goals by not getting the student involved in the decision-making process?

Answer: In a lot of cases, I initially don't talk to the student as much or as directly as I do to parents. Basically, using this approach allows you to get the parents involved and to have them help to solve the student's school-related problems. After the problem is solved, then you can talk all you want to a "successful" student about positive things. Many times, if the student is in difficulty, he is a master of manipulation and can get you and the family off track in terms of the solution to the problem. Therefore, I don't often talk directly to the student about having him come up with solutions to the problems.

For example, if you asked a student how he feels about going to school or why he doesn't go to school, how new or useful is the information that you get? After fifteen or twenty years of doing this type of counseling, you pretty much have heard it all. The issue is this: Is it important to have the student in school? If so, get him to go to school and be successful; then you don't need to talk to the student about his reasons for not going to school or for failing. You don't have to talk to him about why he is flunking, because he is not flunking; he is passing.

This intervention program is basically designed to get the student to act appropriately. After he starts acting appropriately, if you care to talk to him and get involved with him, please do so. But it is recommended that you do so on a positive basis rather than by spending a lot of time with negative issues. This does not mean that you don't care about the student or that you are insensitive to him and are ignoring him. Instead, it means that you have a directed focus—to have the student become successful.

Another dimension of this issue is that the parents are the ones who have the power, and they are the ones who need to have the hierarchy of the family restructured. Up to this time, the student is the one who has been making the decisions and running the family, and that method has not been working out very well—which is the reason why the family needs counseling. You need to help the parents to restore the hierarchy, to put them back in the decision-making mode—especially in this one particular area in the student's life—and to have them deal with the problem and come to a successful resolution. From the student's behavior it appears that missing school or flunking out is *no problem to him*—or he would have taken it upon himself to change his behavior. Therefore, it reverts to the parents to take a stand: What are *they* going to do to solve the problem?

To some individuals' way of thinking, you might be defeating one portion of the therapeutic goal by not having the student involved in the decision-making process, but consider this: imagine yourself debating or arguing with Helen Keller when she was a young girl, asking her what she would like to do, asking her for her decisions, asking her if she would like to use a napkin or to learn to read and write, and asking her how she felt about it—all in an attempt to get her to be successful.

In the initial stage of the counseling process, I don't care to have the student involved in the decision-making process. At this point, the student can't make the decisions. Until he has learned the social customs, internalized the process, and been successful, he may have no choice in the decision. For example, you would not give a two-year-old child the right to make the decision on whether or not to get out of the street. In certain areas, such as in crucial, non-negotiable, "must" behaviors, I'm not interested in the student's decisions. If the behavior is an issue to the parents and they want it changed, then you have to help the parents to get the inappropriate behavior back under control and the student back on the track of being successful. Once the student has internalized the process and learned to be successful, you no longer have a problem. Again, going back to the example of a two-year-old out in the street, once he's out of the street, has learned to stay out of the street, and learned to behave in ways you feel are safe street behaviors, you won't have to worry about his making poor adult decisions because he will basically be making very good decisions. The same thing is true with going to school. When the student is getting good grades and shows up at school all the time, you don't have to worry about the problem of his making poor decisions—because he is not doing so; in fact, he is doing very well.

Toilet-training gives us another example. When the child was being toilet-trained, he was given no choice to make his own decisions. After he had learned to go to the bathroom in the proper place and way, whatever the family's value-system is, then there was no problem with that behavior. From then on, we all look at the child and say, "Well, he makes very good decisions and is independent, grown-up, and mature in this particular area." The reason why we can say this is that he *is* socialized and has learned appropriate, culturally-defined rules and non-negotiable, absolute, "must" bathroom behaviors. I'm not concerned about the child's being involved in the initial decision-making process; I am concerned with his ultimate success. And I believe that the initial parental involvement has no bearing whatsoever on his sense of freedom or his independence or on his sense of internal locus of control. Most of us do not worry about or get upset and anxious about our freedom or locus of control in relation to going to the bathroom at certain times or places. Why? Because we've already been successful for years, and this is not even an issue.

Children who know how to read and write well are much more independent than children who don't. As in the toilet-training example, students who read well don't usually see that as a problem or an issue in terms of their internal locus of control, decision-making process, independence, or freedom. In fact, most of these children believe that they have more of those qualities because they are successful.

Question: What about some of the more severe clinical symptoms and problems, such as suicide, anorexia, and drugs? Can this approach work with these types of problems?

Answer: Yes, this approach can work very well with a lot of these problems. Depending on your expertise, clinical experience, training, and time-and-place appropriateness, you can adapt and modify some of these techniques for these more severe clinical symptoms and problems. However, these problems usually require more time to solve and are better handled in private practice. This particular book is designed to deal with short-term problems—one or two sessions within a school setting. Suicide, anorexia, and other more-severe problems are much more difficult and should be referred to outside resources for more consistent follow-up. If you are in private practice, however, you can use this approach, and it works well.

As a general statement, if the family is fairly clear on the direction in which they are going, the hierarchy is straightened out, the parents are giving clear directions and messages, the child knows where he fits in, and there is a fairly good-feeling tone in the family, then many of these "severe" problems don't seem to emerge. On the other hand, however, if the child is suicidal, discouraged, overly anxious or depressed, you can determine with a fairly high degree of certainty that there are unresolved problems in the family, constant battles and hassles going on, the child doesn't know whether or not he fits in, or the child doesn't know whether or not anyone really cares. If these conditions are present in the family, these difficulties then increase the chances that the person may manifest a wide range of possible clinical symptoms, or symptomatology. There are no guarantees. However, if the hierarchy and communications are clear, there will be, generally speaking, fewer problems and less stress in the family; this reduction will then lead to a lower incidence of these types of clinical symptoms.

Question: How do you respond to the criticism set forth by Jones and Jones (*Comprehensive Classroom Management,* 1986) of assertive discipline, and of your method by implication, when they state, "It seems ironic that teachers so often accept classroom-management methods such as assertive discipline that emphasize immediate control and order but fail to provide children with skills needed to become responsible citizens"? Jones and Jones also suggest that teachers need to employ problem-solving approaches to disciplinary and classroom-management problems rather than rely on authoritarian control. They state that through the problem-solving techniques the student will learn self-responsibility. How do you respond to that?

Answer: In every classroom environment, I think there are two major components or elements that you cannot get away from. One is the amount of control and structure in the classroom; the other is the amount of caring, nurturance, and love that is going on in the classroom. My feeling is that you need to have a high amount of structure, caring, love, and nurturance going on in the educational environment to maximize most student outcomes. After students have learned certain basic skills and have "become responsible", whatever that means by various adult definitions, then you don't need as much "external control" or "structure" and you can let them then be independent, responsible, and "do it on their own." After the student has internalized the structure, the structure is still there, but it is not so overt, apparent, nor so necessary to enforce from external sources. Going back to the analogy of the two-year-old out in the middle of the street, if you want the student to be "responsible" and to learn how to solve problems, then spend the time and energy to teach him and have him internalize the process rather than run the risk of having the child killed while he's learning to make these decisions and being "responsible" on his own. My feeling is that he has no decisional choice on whether or not he is going to be out in the street. *After* he gets the message that there is no way that he is going to be out in the street, *after* he has learned the appropriate behavior and skills associated with safe street behavior, and *after* he has demonstrated that safe behavior for a period of time, then you can back off and let him make "responsible" decisions in safe increments so he's at least alive to tell about it.

The same general principles apply in terms of the school environment. If there is a rule of absolutely no fighting in school and you will not allow a person to physically fight or hurt anybody, then there is no decision in this matter. After the students have learned they have no decision or option in this area, and if normal school-related social problems emerge from living and being together, then, yes, teach them all the skills related to social and responsible behavior. Teach them problem-solving techniques; teach them communication skills and decision-making skills. Let them pay the consequences for their actions but only in safe increments that aren't going to be absolutely harmful and destructive to them. In terms of the caring and nurturance dimension in education, I highly recommend that you teach them all the social and personal skills you can. Teach them how to negotiate for what they need and want and how to get along with other people. Teach them social skills and affective education. Set up the classroom environment in terms of cooperative education. Do all these things and more. I think that's great. There is no doubt that we should incorporate more of these types of things in our schools.

The point is, however, that regardless of these positive, caring elements, I believe the students still need structure, guidance and discipline in our schools. I know of districts and schools that have well-trained staff-members, who are well-intentioned, have a lot of love, and who try to get the kids to be responsible—but the gangs are tearing the places apart. Don't allow these students to make the "decisions". Set the standards, set the rules, set the limits, and stop the crazy, bizarre, inappropriate behaviors. After this crazy behavior has stopped, *then* you can let the students make decisions in the normal ranges of healthy living, experiencing, and exploring. Let them experience coopertive learning and responsibility. Let them pay the consequences for their actions, but set the limits so that these experiences are in a normal healthy range. I'd love to see how Jones and Jones, or other colleagues who spout philosophies like theirs, would deal with inner-city schools where gangs are taking over. I can picture them talking to the students or trying to teach them about their social responsibilities, being nice to each other, and the consequences of hurting each other. These kids have *heard* all of this. The problem is that they are not *doing* any of it.

These situations are similar to parents saying to the child "You should know better than this, and you need to learn to do what school or society requires—or you will have to pay the consequences." To these parents I say, "You're right; he should know better. But he is not doing better. Is that a problem to you, and do you want to change it?" I'd probably use the same technique with Jones and Jones. I would simply ask them, "Well, if the kids aren't doing what you want, is that a problem to you, and, if so, what would you do about it?" If it's not a problem, then let the students continue acting out, and see if they "adjust", "learn", and become "responsible". My hunch is that it might take the students a long time to learn, if they learn at all.

On the other hand, if you stop or cut down on most inappropriate behavior quickly by taking an authoritative stand, then when people aren't feeling so mad, nasty, hurt, and revengeful, they will have a better chance of being more polite and more responsible to each other. When the craziness stops, then the social-skills training and other caring, humanistic philosophies can emerge and have a chance of surviving, growing, and developing in the education environment.

Question: What are the major differences between this approach Brief Family Intervention (BFI) and, say, (a) tough love, (b) assertive discipline, (c) Glasser's reality therapy or control theory, (d) Dreikur's logical and natural consequences or some other form of adlerian psychology, and (e) Dobson's approach?

Answer: The major difference between this approach and the others is that all of them philosophically operate from a one-person model and give the choice to the child. It's the identified student or patient who has the problem; it's his responsibility to deal with the issues. In the family-systems model, the basic assumption is a three-person model where the family's values and interactions are studied to see how they contribute to, maintain the symptoms of, or otherwise keep the problem operating. This is the major underlying difference between those approaches and the one described in this book. Here are some comparisons in terms of some of the specific philosophical issues and differences:

Tough Love. My understanding of Tough Love is that basically at some point or another parents get to a point where they say, "These are the rules, and if you don't follow them, then you can leave." They then give the child some options on where he can go. Basically I look at this perspective as an if/then contract. The difference between Tough Love's message and BFI's message is that BFI proposes that (1) we are going to tell the child clearly and specifically what the rules are and (2) then take whatever action is necessary to stop the inappropriate behavior and achieve the stated goal. We are not going to give the child the message that "If you don't like it, you can leave." Rather, we will give the message that "We care about you, we love you very much, we won't allow you to do this inappropriate behavior, and we'll take whatever steps necessary to help prevent that. You are part of this family, we're going to work this out together. You cannot leave. We will deal with the problems and issues as a family, and we will solve them."

This approach is *not* like Tough Love, in which you can say, "If things get tough, you may check out, leave, or go somewhere else." The message from BFI is clearly, "We will work it out."

Assertive Discipline. The major difference with Assertive Discipline is, again, if/then contracts. Assertive Discipline goes through a wide range of if/then contracts, from checkmarks on the board to marbles in a glass jar to various rewards or negative consequences.

Again, philosophically, BFI says, "No, you're not going to have any choice in this particular area. We're not going to give you a choice of consequences. You have no other choice but to do the required behavior, which is to stop the inappropriate behavior." Also, with BFI, we bring in the family for a family-systems counseling session if the interventions which we used in the school don't seem to work. Assertive Discipline basically does not incorporate a three-person, family-systems counseling approach or model.

Glasser's Reality Therapy. There are basically two major differences between Glasser's Reality Therapy/Control Theory and BFI. The first is that BFI is a systems approach which deals specifically with the family rather than with just the individual student. The second is that Glasser's Reality Therapy/Control Theory has the student describe what it is he has done wrong, asks him if that is what he has said he would do in terms of a previous contract or committment, and then negotiates with the student to set up a new contract in the hope of making him responsible for his own behavior. Philosophically, I enjoy Glasser's model and accept many of the ideas set forth by him to be valid ones. However, if you have a child who is acting-out inappropriately, if you don't have a lot of time to allow the child to continue to act inappropriately until he wishes to act responsibly, and if you don't want him to do extreme types of inappropriate behavior, then you need to involve the family and take a stand to put a stop to the behavior.

After the student has stopped the crazy, acting-out behavior and is more successful, it is possible that within that milder and more normal range of growth and development the child can pay the consequences of his actions and be responsible.

In terms of Glasser's Control Theory, he believes that, again, the student has to be internally oriented or motivated and choose to act appropriately. Part of me philosophically accepts this position, but there's another part of me that says that's not true. When it comes to certain core elements or non-negotiables, if the student chooses not to want to do or follow the rules on his own, then you have to give him the structure to make it happen for a period of time, until he chooses to or learns to choose to want to do it on his own.

Dreikur's Adlerian Psychology Approach: Logic and Natural Consequences. Some Adlerians say that the BFI model can be explained from their logic-and-natural-consequence model. For example, a father going out on a date with a daughter to have her home or in the house by midnight would be interpreted as "the consequence" of the daughter's previous decisions or actions. In a way you can conceptualize it that way, which is fine with me. I don't particularly care how you conceptualize results; I'm more interested in whether or not the results are acheived.

Philosophically, the differences are these: (1) BFI is a family-systems approach, and (2) most of the "consequences" that Adlerians claim are actually if/then contracts of the success-or-failure type rather than of the success-or-success type of BFI. Instead of the message's being "If you don't do this, then you will pay this consequence", BFI is a "must" contract.

Under the "must" contract, there is no other choice, and we'll do whatever we need to do in order to make sure that it happens, to make sure that you are successful. We're not interested in punishing you or having you pay the consequences for your poor decisions. We're not interested in having you pay the natural consequences of standing out in the middle of the street—and getting run over and killed— just so that you can learn to pay the price. We're not interested in having you eat all the sugar you want and not brushing your teeth—and having your teeth rot out. No, you have no choice in these areas of your life. Basically, after years of successfully brushing your teeth after meals and after years of successful socialization and habit-formation, then, yes, you can have freedom to make choices on your own in these areas.

Dobson's Approach. I enjoy Dobson's approach, and I like his humor, but philosophically I feel uncomfortable with part of Dobson's approach. In *Dare to Discipline* and in his film series, he recommends that, when all else fails, the parent grab hold of the child by the neck along some nerve and press the heck out of it. This brings tears to the child's eyes and can drop someone to his knees almost immediately. In one of his films, he kiddingly says that if the kid is taller than you are and if you have to reach your hand above your head to grab hold of this nerve, it's probably best not to do so. Of course, this gets a good laugh from the audience at the time, but the point is that it's just another way of punishing and hurting children. Dobson falls back into the same punishment trap, in this case "if you don't do it this way, then I'm going to punish you by grabbing you by the neck and squeezing it until you drop to your knees".

Occasionally, you may have to use some form of punishment during child-rearing. However, this method advocates that punishment is not something you should choose to want to do from a philosophical perspective. If you could do anything else to get the child to do what you wanted him to do, wouldn't you rather do that than have to hurt the child in some way? I would much rather operate from the perspective that says "I am going to give you a clear message that says that in this one particular area of your life there is no choice. I'll do whatever I can to make you successful. I might have to use some creative back-ups or constraints to accomplish this goal, but I'm not going to do anything to physically harm you."

Again, what I would like parents and teachers to do is to be critical thinkers. Explore, challenge, and evaluate different approaches, and see which one works to accomplish the intended goals. I'm relatively pragmatic—if it works, it works; if there is no problem, then there is no problem. In all the approaches that I have studied, learned, or dealt with over the years, I have found some useful elements and ideas from each. There are useful elements in every approach, and I encourage you to use the ones which work. Become eclectic in terms of your ideas and your approaches; use different techniques for different children or students. Remember: If it works, it works.

Also, remember the premise that you don't have to bring out cannons to get kids to eat peas. Use the smallest amount of control, restriction, limit-setting, or authoritative demands that you need to get the child to be successful. Try different approaches. Use successful elements, components, or techniques of the different methods. Be polite, be sociable, and encourage the child to act appropriately; but again, if all else fails, then use this particular method. Conceptually, I see the BFI approach, or method, used to deal with or stop crazy, bizarre, inappropriate behavior and to quickly get the student back under control. After the child is under relative control and is acting in a more normal manner, then, if needed, the other approaches or therapies may be the methods of choice. These other approaches used within more normal, educational, and developmental ranges are more what I call the "quality-of-life" types of therapies—getting kids to be generally more responsible, getting them to understand things, training or teaching them social skills, and so forth. Under these circumstances, when children are acting fairly appropriately and within a normal range of acceptable behaviors, you don't need to be heavy-handed and make the decisions for the students. However, when students are beyond the normal range of acceptable behavioral limits, you should take an active stance to stop or prevent the student's inappropriate behavior.

Chapter VIII: Summary

As a summary and final statement, I would like to say this: Love your children, care about them, respect them, do as much as possible to have them grow and develop, teach them social skills, and teach them how to identify and express their feelings and to become uniquely human; but, at the same time, care about them enough and love them enough to give them guidance, structure, limits, and control as they need it. If, by being successful and acting appropriately, they demonstrate to you that they don't need this structure, then you don't need to give them so much. Part of the role of parenting and of being a parent is to care enough so that if the child needs the structure and guidance, you're willing to give it. It means that you are willing to set the boundaries and guidelines so that the child can use that structure to grow in a responsible, productive way and to learn to control himself and learn to make positive, health-producing, successful choices.

The bottom-line message is to care about your children and students, love them, but expect something out of them. Expect them to have manners. Expect them to achieve and perform well, both academically and behaviorally. Don't be afraid to expect those things. Don't be afraid of setting reasonable rules and standards, and don't be afraid to impose limits, clear structure, guidance, and controls. Most of the cases that have been presented in this book and in *How to Deal with Discipline Problems in the Schools* have been at the far side of the control variable, and you saw more of the control and authoritative side of the caring and loving dimension in an effort to stop crazy and self-destructive behaviors. My feeling is that an ounce of precaution is worth a pound of cure. If the child knows that you love him and he learns early that you are the parent, that you mean what you say, that you are consistent and will give him structure, guidance, and limits when he needs them, then most of the time you won't ever need to use this type of approach.

My wish for parents and teachers is that things are going so well in your family or school that you wouldn't need to use this approach. If the child is acting appropriately and is doing well, then there is no problem and no need to use these extreme measures. However, if the child is not acting appropriately and you do have some problems, then you need to do something to stop the inappropriate behavior. *You need to care enough to be a parent, to be a teacher.*

Appendix A: Bibliography of Family Therapy

OVERVIEWS

Goldenberg, Irene, and Goldenberg, H. *Family Therapy: An Overview.* Monterey, California: Brooks/Cole, 1980.
_____. *A Family Therapy Workbook.* Monterey, California: Brooks/Cole, 1980.
Jones, Susan. *Family Therapy: A Comparison of Approaches.* Englewood Cliffs, N.J.: Robert Brady Co./Prentice-Hall, 1980.
Levant, Ronald. *Family Therapy: A Comprehensive Overview.* Englewood Cliffs, N.J.: Prentice-Hall, 1984.

BLENDED and STEP-FAMILIES

Ahrons, C.R., and Perlmutter, M.S. "The Relationship Between Former Spouses: A Fundamental Sub-system in the Remarriage Family." In J.C. Hansen & L. Messinger (eds.), *Therapy with Remarriage Families.* Rockville, Maryland: Aspen Systems Corporation, 1982.
Duberman, L. *The Reconstituted Family: A Study of Remarried Couples and Their Children.* Chicago: Nelson-Hall, 1975.
Goldner, V. "Remarriage Family: Structure, System, Future." In J.C. Hansen & L. Messinger (eds.) *Therapy with Remarriage Families.* Rockville, Maryland: Aspen Systems Corporation, 1982.
McGoldrick, M., and Carter, E.A. "Forming a Remarried Family." In E.A. Carter & M. McGoldrick (eds.) *The Family Life Cycle: A Framework for Family Therapy.* New York: Gardner Press, 1980.
Messinger, L., Walker, K.N., and Freeman, S.J.I. "Preparation for Remarriage Following Divorce: The Use of Group Techniques." *American Journal of Orthopsychiatry,* 48(2), 263-272, 1978.
Ransom, J.W., Schlesinger, S., and Derdeyn, A.A. "A Step-family in Formation." *American Journal of Orthopsychiatry,* 49(1), 36-43, 1979.

Sager, C. J., Brown, H.S., Crohn, H., Engel, T., Rodstein, E., and Walker, L. *Treating the Remarried Family.* New York: Brunner/Mazel, 1983.

Visher, E.B., and Visher, J.S. *Step-families: A Guide to Working with Step-parents and Step-children.* New York: Brunner/Mazel, 1979.

——————. *How to Win as a Step-family.* New York: Brunner/Mazel, 1982.

Wald, E. *The Remarried Family: Challenge and Promise.* New York: Family Service Association of America, 1981.

Wallerstein, J.S., and Kelly, J.B. *Surviving the Breakup: How Children and Parents Cope with Divorce.* New York: Basic Books, 1980.

STRUCTURAL FAMILY THERAPY

Baker, Lester, Minuchin, S, and Liebman, R. "Anorexia Nervosa: Successful Application of a Family Therapy Approach." *Pediatric Research,* No. 7 (1973), pp. 294-299.

Flomenhaft, Kalman, and Carter, Ross E. "Family Therapy Training: Program and Outcome." *Family Process: A Multidisciplinary Journal of Family Study Research and Treatment,* Vol. 16, No.2, (June 1977), pp. 211-218.

Liebman, Ronald and Minuchin, Salvador. "The Use of Structural Family Therapy in the Treatment of Intractable Asthma." *American Journal of Psychiatry* (1974), pp. 535-540.

Minuchin, Salvador. *Families of the Slums: An Exploration of Their Structure and Treatment,* with B. Montalvo and B.C. Guerney, Jr., et. al. New York: Basic Books, 1967.

——————. *Families and Family Therapy.* Cambridge: Harvard University Press, 1974.

——————. Rosman, B.L., and Baker, L. *Psychosomatic Families.* Cambridge: Harvard University Press, 1978.

——————. and Fishman, H.C. *Family Therapy Techniques.* Cambridge: Harvard University Press, 1981.

——————. et.al. "A Conceptual Model of Psychosomatic Illness in Children." *Archives of General Psychiatry,* Vol. 32 (August 1975), pp. 1031-1038.

——————. "Plight of the Poverty-Stricken Family in the United States Today." *Child Welfare,* Vol. XLIX, No. 3 (1970), pp.124-130.

——————. "Techniques for Working with Disorganized Low Socioeconomic Families." *American Journal of Orthopsychiatry,* Vol. 37, No. 5 (October 1967), pp. 881-887.

——————. and Barchai, Avner. "Therapeutically Induced Family Crisis." *Science and Psychoanalysis,* Vol. 19 (1969), pp. 199-205.

Montalvo, Braulio. "Aspects of Live Supervision." *Family Process: A Multidisciplinary Journal of Family Study and Treatment,* Vol. 12, No.1 (December 1973), pp. 343-359.

Ziegler-Driscoll, Genevra. "Family Research Study at Eagleville Hospital and Rehabilitation Center." *Family Process: A Multidisci-*

plinary Journal of Family Study and Research and Treatment, Vol. 16, No. 2 (June 1977), pp. 175-190.

FUNCTIONAL FAMILY THERAPY

Alexander, James, and Parsons, Bruce. *Functional Family Therapy.* Monterey, California: Brooks/Cole, 1982.

Alexander, J. F. "Defensive and Supportive Communications in Normal and Deviant Families." *Journal of Consulting and Clinical Psychology,* 1973, 40(2), 223-231.

_____. "Behavior Modification and Delinquent Youth." In J.C. Cull & R. E. Hardy (eds.) *Behavior Modification in Rehabilitation Settings.* Springfield, Illinois: Charles C. Thomas, 1974.

Alexander, J. F., and Barton, C. "Behavioral Systems Therapy with Families." In D. H. Olson (ed.) *Treating Relationships.* Lake Mills, Iowa: Graphic, 1976.

_____. "Systems-Behavioral Intervention with Delinquent Families." In J. Vincent (ed.) *Advances in Family Intervention, Assessment, and Theory.* Greenwich, Connecticut: JAI Press, 1980.

_____. Schiavo, R.S., and Parsons, B.V. "Behavioral Intervention with Families of Delinquents: Therapist Characteristics and Outcome.' *Journal of Consulting and Clinical Psychology,* 1976, 44(4), 656-664.

Alexander, J. F., and Parsons, B.V. "Short-term Behavioral Intervention with Delinquent Families: Impact on Family Process and Recidivism." *Journal of Abnormal Psychology,* 1973, 81(3), 219-225.

Barton, C., and Alexander, J.F. "Treatment of Families with a Delinquent Member." In G. Harris (ed.) *The Group Treatment of Human Problems: A Source Learning Approach.* New York: Grune & Stratton, 1977.

_____. "Systems-Behavioral Family Therapy." In A. S. Gurman & D. P. Kniskern (eds.) *Handbook of Family Therapy.* New York: Brunner/Mazel, 1980.

STRATEGIC FAMILY THERAPY

Haley, Jay. *Leaving Home.* New York: McGraw-Hill, 1980.

_____. *Ordeal Therapy.* San Francisco: Jossey-Bass, 1976.

_____. *Problem-Solving Therapy.* San Francisco: Jossey-Bass, 1976.

_____. *Strategies of Psychotherapy.* New York: Grune & Stratton, 1963.

_____. and Lynn Hoffman. *Techniques of Family Therapy.* New York: Basic Books, 1968.

_____. *Uncommon Therapy: The Psychiatric Techniques of Milton H. Erickson, M.D.* New York: W.W. Norton & Co., 1977.

_____. *The Power Tactics of Jesus Christ.* Rockville, Maryland: The Triangle Press, 1986.

Madanes, Cloe. *Behind the One-Way Mirror.* San Francisco: Jossey-Bass, 1984.

―――――. *Strategic Family Therapy.* San Francisco: Jossey-Bass, 1981.

BRIEF THERAPY IN SCHOOLS BASED ON STRATEGIC THERAPY

Bowman, P., and Goldberg, M. " 'Reframing': A Tool for the School Psychologist." *Psychology in the Schools,* Vol. 20 (April 1983), pp. 210-214.

DeShazer, S. *Keys to Solution in Brief Therapy.* New York: W.W. Norton & Co., 1985.

Fisch, R., Weakland, J., and Segal, L. *The Tactics of Change: Doing Therapy Briefly.* (1983), San Francisco: Jossey-Bass.

Kral, R. "Indirect Therapy in the Schools." In deShazer, S. (ed.) *Indirect Approaches in Therapy.* Family Therapy Collections, Vol. 19, 1986, Rockville, Maryland: Aspen Systems Corporation.

GENERAL BIBLIOGRAPHY

Ackerman, N.W. *The Psychodynamics of Family Life.* New York: Basic Books, 1958.

Becker, Wesley. "Consequences of Difficult Kinds of Parental Discipline." In M.L. Hoffman (eds.) *Review of Child Development Research* (Vol. I). New York: Russell Sage Foundation, 1964.

Boszormenyi-Nagy, I., and Framo, J.L. (eds.) *Intensive Family Therapy: Theoretical and Practical Aspects.* New York: Harper & Row, 1965.

Coopersmith, Stanley. *The Antecedents of Self-esteem.* San Francisco and London: W.H. Freeman & Co., 1967.

Dave, Ravjndrakumar. *The Identification and Measurement of Environmental Process Variables that are Related to Educational Achievement* (Doctoral dissertation, University of Chicago, 1963, #T10342).

Erickson, Gerald D., and Hogan, T.P. *Family Therapy: An Introduction to Theory and Technique.* Monterey, California: Brooks/Cole, 1972.

Framo, J. (ed.) *Family Interaction: A Dialogue Between Family Researchers and Family Therapists.* New York: Springer, 1980.

Jackson, Don D. (ed.) *Communication, Family & Marriage.* (The Human Communication Series: Vol. I). Palo Alto, California: Science & Behavior Books, 1968.

―――――. *Therapy, Communication, and Change* LC 68-21577. (The Human Communication Series: Vol. 2.) Palo Alto, California: Science & Behavior Books, 1968.

Jackson, Don D. (ed.) *The Etiology of Schizophrenia.* New York: Basic Books, 1960

Jones, V, and Jones, L. *Comprehensive Classroom Management.* Boston: Allyn & Bacon, 1986).

McGoldbrick, M., and Gerson, R. *Genograms in Family Assessment.* New York: W.W. Norton & Co., 1968.

McInnis, Phil. *Assured Readiness for Learning.* Author, Rte. 364, 2452 Potter Road, Penn Yan, N.Y. 14527.

Napier, A., and Whitaker, C. *The Family Crucible.* New York: Harper & Row, 1978.

Neill, John, and Kiskern, D. *From Psyche to System: The Evolving Therapy of Carl Whitaker.* New York: The Guilford Press, 1982.

Okun, B. F., and Rappaport, L.J. *Working with Families: An Introduction to Family Therapy.* North Scituate, Mass.: Duxbury, 1980.

Palazolli, S., Boscolo, L., Cecchin, G., and Prata, G. *Paradox and Counterparadox.* New York: Jason Aronson, 1978.

Papp, P. *Family Therapy: Full-Length Case Studies.* New York: Gardner Press, 1977.

Patterson, G. R., et.al. *A Social Learning Approach to Family Intervention, Vol. I: Families with Aggressive Children.* Eugene, Oregon: Castalia Publications, 1975.

Petrie, Patricia, and Piersel, Wayne C. "Family Therapy". In C.R. Reynolds & T.B. Gutkin (eds.) *The Handbook of School Psychology.* New York: John Wiley & Sons, 1982.

Satir, Virginia, et.al. *Changing with Families.* Palo Alto, California: Science & Behavior Books, 1975.

_____. *Helping Families to Change.* New York: Jason Aronson, 1975.

Satir, Virginia. *Conjoint Family Therapy.* Palo Alto, California: Science & Behavior Books, 1967.

Schaefer, Earl S. "Parents as Educators: Evidence from Cross-sectional, Longitudinal, and Intervention Research." In Willard W. Hartup (ed.) *The Young Child: Reviews of Research, Vol. 2.* Washington, D.C.: Institute of Child Development, University of Minnesota National Association for Education of Young Children, 1972.

Schroder, Carole A., and Crawford, Pat. *The Relationship of the Home to Under- or Over-achievement.* Toronto Board of Education Research Department, January 1971. (ERIC Document Reproduction Service No. ED-079626.)

Stanton, M.D., and Todd, T.C. *The Family Therapy of Drug Abuse and Addiction.* New York: Guilford Press, 1982.

_____. Structural Family Therapy with Drug Addicts. In E. Kaufman and P. Kaufman (eds.) *The Family Therapy of Drug and Alcohol Abuse.* New York: Gardner Press, 1979.

Thompson, Mark E. *Distinctive Characteristics of Over- and Underachieving Students: A Synthesis of the Research Literature.* Lexington, Kentucky, 1976. (ERIC Document Reproduction Service No. ED-131358.)

Valentine, Michael R. *An Exploratory Study of Family Background Variables in Relation to Academic Performance, Persistence, Intel-*

lectual Orientation, Locus of Control, and Self-Concept (Doctoral dissertation, University of California Los Angeles, 1980.)

Visher, E., and Visher, J. *Step-Families.* New York: Brunner/ Mazel, 1979.

Watzlawick, P., Beavin, J.H., and Jackson, D.D. *Pragmatics of Human Communication.* New York: W.W. Norton & Co., 1967.

Watzlawick, P., and Weakland, J.H. (eds.). *The Interactional View: Studies at the Mental Research Institute, Palo Alto, 1965-1974.* New York: W.W. Norton & Co., 1977.

Weeks, G., and L'Abate, L. *Paradoxical Psychotherapy: Theory and Practice with Individual, Couples, & Families.* New York: Brunner/ Mazel, 1982.

Whitaker, C. (ed.). *Psychotherapy of Chronic Schizophrenic Patients.* Boston: Little, Brown, 1958.

RECOMMENDED PARENT BOOKS BASED ON THIS MODEL

Bodenhamer, Greg. *Back in Control.* Englewood Cliffs, N.J.: Prentice-Hall, 1984.

Wood, P., and Schwartz, B. *How To Get Your Children To Do What You Want Them To Do.* Englewood Cliffs, N.J.: Prentice-Hall, 1977.

Valentine, Michael R. *How to Deal with Discipline Problems in the Schools.* Austin: Educational Directions Incorporated, 1987.

RECOMMENDED TAPES

The Evolution of Psychotherapy. Infomedix Educational Resources/ 12800 Garden Grove Blvd., Suite E/Garden Grove/CA 92643.

Don Jackson Memorial Conference Tapes, Infomedix Educational Resources/12800 Garden Grove Blvd., Suite E/Garden Grove/CA 92643.

Appendix B: Parental Outline for Dealing with Discipline Problems

I. *Set the Goal and the Standards*

What must the child do or stop doing so that you will think that the problem is solved? State the rules and the solution to the problem in very clear, concrete, specific, objective, observable, behavioral terms, such as: go to school; get to school on time; stay in school all day; do all your school work at school, neatly and correctly; get nothing less than straight C's in all subjects for the rest of your school career; turn in all assignments on time; and don't hit anyone.

Planned Parental Response—What is the problem? Describe the inappropriate behavior in clear behavioral terms:

_____
_____
_____
_____

(See Appendix C for more information and helpful hints for parents to set the goal.)

REMEMBER: Stay focused on solving this problem and having the child achieve this goal. Do not get manipulated by the child ("your value-system is over the hill", "you don't love me as much as you love my sister") or get side-tracked by other such issues ("Are you a 'good' parent?").

II. Let the Child Know the Rules, Goals, and Standards
   A. Let the child know of any previous excuses or beliefs that you had about his assumed "incapabilities".
   B. Let the child know that you *no longer* believe these excuses because there is specific evidence to the contrary.
   C. Tell the child the new rules, goals, and standards.
   D. Let the child know that you love him and will do whatever it takes to make sure that he achieves these goals, even if he initially chooses not to do them on his own.

Planned Parent Response

   A. Write out any previous *beliefs* and *excuses:*
   _____
   _____

   B. Write out *evidence* to the contrary:
   _____
   _____

   C. State new rules, goals, and standards:
   _____
   _____

   D. Let the child know that you love him but that from now on you expect him to be successful in this area and you will do whatever it takes to make this happen:
   _____
   _____

REMEMBER: It is helpful if you practice saying statements A-D aloud a few times before you relate them to the child. Doing this will help you to make sure that your message is clear and specific enough.

Appendix B: Parental Outline   *191*

III. *General Plan When Child Does Not Comply*

    A. First intervention strategy: What will you say when he doesn't do the stated behavior?
_____
_____

Anticipated response of the child (*e.g.,* anger, pouting, swearing, fighting back) to your clear message:
_____

    B. Second intervention strategy: What will you say and do if the child does not respond to the first intervention?
_____
_____

Anticipated response of child: _____

    C. Third intervention strategy: What will you do and say now? _____
_____

REMEMBER: Stay focused on the solution to the problem. Do not get side-tracked by other issues or develop some new elaborate form of punishment. Work on expressing yourself clearly and with firm caring and concern.

IV. *Development of Back-up Support*

    General Plan: If initial interventions do not work, what do you need to do to back up your statements to make the child successful? Who do you need to help you? Develop a plan with these individuals. Write out your plan:
_____
_____
_____
_____

Whose help do you need? Check off on the list:
- ___ Support from spouse: The two of you have talked it over, agreed on a plan, and are willing to support each other for the child's well-being even if you strongly disagree with each other in other areas of your relationship.
- ___ Support from other family members, such as sisters and brothers, grandparents, inlaws, and cousins.
- ___ Support from hired aides, such as tutors, body-guards, and escorts.
- ___ Support from school personnel, such as principal, teachers, librarian, bus-driver, custodian, and lunch aides.
- ___ Support from neighbors if needed and if appropriate.
- ___ Support from church or community support groups and agencies if needed and if appropriate.
- ___ Support from the police department, probation department, social workers, and court systems if needed and if appropriate.

REMEMBER: Devise back-up techniques that say, "I love you and care about you so much that I will not let you fail, hurt yourself, or make a poor decision in this one area of your life. I will not hurt you, punish you, or belittle you. However, I *will* do whatever is necessary to make sure that you are successful." The choice of a good back-up technique is a choice between success and success, not between success and failure. The bottom-line message conveyed to the child is this: "You must do the desired behavior. There is no way out of doing it." You—the parents—must be willing to put in the time and energy to make the goal-behavior happen. You must be consistent, monitor the behavior, and follow through. You must convey to the child that you have a 100% committment to this goal—and the goal will be achieved. There is no choice—it will happen.

Appendix C: Helpful Suggestions for Getting Your Child to do What You Want Him to Do

A. *Decide on the Specific Behaviors of the Child that Are To Be Changed:*
  1. It is better if both parents agree and are willing to support each other on this.
  2. Make the goal clear and specific: Go to school each day, stay in school, do all your work, and get nothing less than straight C's instead of "He has an attitude problem" or "I want him to work up to his potential."
  3. Break the goal into manageable units: "Do these 10 math problems neatly and correctly within the next 15 minutes; then I will check them with you.").
  4. Monitor behavior. If the student is not being successful, that is a clear message that he needs more help and guidance from you to insure that he is successful.

B. *Obstacles to Clear Demands:*
  1. Am I sure that he is capable of this behavior?
     a. What possible "excuses" for him have I been entertaining? Possibilities include: hyperactive, normal behavior "boys will be boys", stages of development, "terrible two's", his friends make him do it, he can't help himself, he's bored, he is just like his Dad, it's because of the divorce.
     b. What objective, observable evidence do I have to support these "excuses" to determine if, in fact, they are true?

c. Have I ever seen my child do this goal behavior before? If so, then he is capable of doing it again.
2. Am I sure that this is a reasonable and essential goal?
   a. Am I willing to let the child make the decision on this (negotiable *vs.* non-negotiable)?
   b. If I am willing to let the child make the decision, can I do it without resentment, hostility, anger, or blaming?
   c. Am I willing to put in the time and energy to follow through on this goal?
3. How is this child going to try to manipulate me? Possibilities include: arguing, crying, pouting, asks "why", questions parenting skills or rights, tantrums, threatens to run away or kill myself.
   a. Did I do this as a child? How did I react to my parents' attempts to deal with my manipulations?
   b. What will I say, and how might I deal with these manipulations? (What is our plan?)

C. *Remember that the Bottom Line Is:*

What is a very clear, specific, concrete, direct message and follow-up technique that tells the child that I love him so much that I will not allow him to be unsuccessful, that he must do this behavior, and that there is no way out of doing what is requested?

D. *Types of Vague Communications to Stay Away from:*
   1. Ignoring inappropriate behavior, hoping it will go away.
   2. Demanding honesty, concern, or sorrow vs. stopping the inappropriate behavior.
   3. Requesting that the child try to change, think about the behavior, or not get caught doing the behavior.
   4. Using abstract terms such as "use common sense", "respect", "grow up", "maturity", "potential", "love", and so on.
   5. Statements of fact: "I see that you didn't take out the trash."
   6. Labeling or classifying. "You're a thief... a bad boy... a baby...", and so on
   7. Questions such as these: "How many times do I have to tell you?" "Why are you hitting your sister?"

8. Wishes, wants and shoulds.
9. If/then contracts. "If you don't do your homework, then you can't go to the dance."
10. Reasoning, inspiring, explaining, lecturing.

REMEMBER: Tell them once, then back it up—which means, do whatever it takes to get the child to do what you want him to do without punishing him or giving him a chance to fail. Care and love him enough to do what is necessary to make him successful.

Appendix D: Glossary

blended family: A reconstituted family formed by the marriage of divorced persons, establishing step-parent relationships as children from previous families merge into a new family unit.
boundaries: Delineations between parts of a system or between systems, such as between grandparents, parents, and children.
coalition: An alliance of factions for some specific purpose, such as mother and children against alcoholic father.
complementary relationship: A pattern of communication between people characterized by inequality and the maximization of differences (for example, dominant/submissive).
conductor: A type of family therapist who is active, aggressive, colorful, and typically becomes the center of the family's star-shaped verbal communication pattern.
conjoint: A single therapist working with family members simultaneously and together.
developmental tasks: Problems to be overcome and conflicts mastered at various stages of the life-cycle, enabling movement on to the next stage of development.
disengagement: Family interaction in which members are isolated and unrelated to each other, each functioning separately and autonomously.
double-bind messages: A set of contradictory messages from the same person to which an individual must respond, although his or her failure to please is inevitable whatever response is made.
dyad: A liaison, temporary or permanent, between two people.

dysfunctional: Abnormal or impaired in functioning.
enmeshment: An extreme form of proximity and intensity in family interactions in which members are overconcerned and overinvolved in each other's life.
extended family: An enlarged and complex family unit in which a married couple and their children plus relatives of other generations (for example, grandparents, uncles, aunts) make up the family structure, all living together or in proximity to one another.
functional family therapy: A family-therapy approach, identified with Alexander, directed at changing the family's interactions by understanding the functions and pay-offs of the behavior.
general systems theory: The study of the relationship of interactional parts in context, emphasizing their unity and organizational hierarchy.
generational boundaries: The natural (psychological) distance (differences) between members of separate generations.
hierarchy: Within a system, an arranged order of parts within the whole.
homeostasis: The self-maintenance of a system in balance or equilibrium.
identified patient: The family member with the presenting symptoms.
life-cycle: The career or history of an individual or group (for example, a family) from its beginning to its termination, usually, accented by noddle points or typical transition points that all people or families go through, such as courting, marriage, birth of first child, and so forth.
live supervision: The active guidance of a therapist while at work by an observing person behind a one-way mirror who offers suggestions by telephone, earphone, or by calling the therapist out of the consultation room.
metacommunication: A communication at a second level that structures and adds meaning to what is said at the first, or surface, level (for example, a communication, such as a nonverbal nod, wink, or smile, that qualifies a verbal message).
paradoxical intervention: A clinical intervention technique whereby a therapist gives a patient or family a

directive he or she wants resisted; the resulting change takes place as a result of defying the therapist.
parentification: The taking on of the nurturing, teaching role of a parent by a child, temporarily or permanently.
reactor: A type of family therapist who is subtle and indirect, observing and clarifying the family group process, rather than an active, aggressive, or colorful group leader.
reframing: Verbal relabeling in order to make seemingly dysfunctional behavior be designated as reasonable and understandable, so that the behavior can be reacted to differently.
scape-goating: The assigning of a "bad" or "guilty" label onto a family member who is held responsible by all for family dysfunction.
strategic family therapy: A family-therapy approach, identified with Haley and Madanes, directed at changing the family's hierarchy and behavior by strategic directions.
structural family therapy: A family-therapy approach, identified with Minuchin, directed at changing the family organization or structure in order to alter behavior patterns in its members; the therapist changes the system by actively participating in its interpersonal transactions.
symbiosis: The close association or interdependence of two persons, the union being advantageous to both and to the maintenance of the family system.
symmetrical relationship: A pattern of communication between people characterized by equality and the minimization of difference.
transgenerational issues: Unresolved problems and issues from the parent's and grandparent's generations that now have a bearing on the problems or symptoms of the identified patient.
triangle: The tendency of a two-person emotional system, under stress, to recruit a third person into an expanded system in order to lower the intensity and anxiety and to gain stability.
triangulation: The act of involving an outsider when two persons are in tension situations.